WASHINGTON INJURY LAW

A REFERENCE GUIDE FOR ACCIDENT VICTIMS

by Christopher M. Davis, Esq.

Special Thanks

This book is a collaborative effort compiled by myself and other leading members of the plaintiff's bar in the states of New York, North Carolina, South Carolina, Texas, Pennsylvania, Arkansas, Florida, Georgia, Indiana, Kentucky, and Tennessee. I want to thank each of the attorneys listed below who have contributed his or her expertise to this project. Each lawyer's contribution has helped make this book a credible and reliable resource regarding the rights and remedies available to accident victims. This is not a law book, but an overview of personal injury law.

Lewis & Daggett, Attorneys at Law, P.A.
North Carolina | www.LewisDaggett.com
Law Offices of Michael A. DeMayo, L.L.P.
North and South Carolina | www.DeMayoLaw.com
Terry Bryant Accident & Injury Law
Texas | www.TerryBryant.com
Rainwater, Holt & Sexton, P.A.
Arkansas | www.CallRainwater.com
Parr Richey Obremskey Frandsen & Patterson
Indiana | www.ParrInjury.com
Martin, Harding & Mazzotti, LLP Attorneys at Law
New York & Vermont | www.1800LAW1010.com
Hagelgans & Veronis
Pennsylvania | www.HVLawfirm.com
Steinger, Iscoe & Greene Injury Lawyers
Florida | www.InjuryLawyers.com
Stokes & Kopitsky P.A.
Georgia | www.StokesInjuryLawyers.com
John Bales Attorneys
Florida | www.JohnBales.com
Hughes & Coleman Injury Lawyers
Kentucky & Tennessee | www.HughesandColeman.com

Additional Editors/Writers:
Sandra K. Rigby
Lorelei Laird

Disclaimer

This publication is designed to provide general information regarding personal injury claims and is not intended to be legal advice. It is sold and distributed with the understanding that neither the publisher, nor the author, nor the contributors, are engaged in rendering legal or other professional services to the reader. If legal advice or other professional assistance is required, the services of a competent professional should be sought.

The publisher, author and contributors make no representations or warranties with respect to the accuracy or completeness of the contents of this work and specifically disclaim all warranties, including without limitation warranties of fitness for a particular purpose. No warranty may be created by sales or promotional materials. The advice and strategies contained herein may not be suitable for every situation. Neither the publisher, nor the authors, nor the contributors shall be liable for damages arising herefrom.

As this publication is not intended as legal advice, any use of this information will not create an attorney-client relationship. After an initial consultation, and before representing you on any claim, a written attorney-client agreement must be signed in order to create such a relationship as required by the attorney ethics rules for the state of Washington.

-

Table of Contents

Foreword

If you're reading this book, you or someone you love has probably been involved in a serious accident. That accident may have caused serious injuries, along with severe pain and emotional trauma. Perhaps you expect to deal with those injuries for the rest of your life—or maybe you're not sure, and you're anxious about your future and your family's future.

To make matters worse, chances are good that the accident caused you to miss work, which has taken a toll on your income. Maybe you're not sure you'll ever be able to do the same job again. Perhaps you're struggling to make ends meet without that income, and that's without worrying about the past and future medical bills resulting from the accident. Maybe the insurance company isn't helping, or you suspect it isn't telling you everything. The entire situation is overwhelming and you know you need help, but you have no idea what to do next.

If this sounds familiar, I wrote this book for you. I intended the book to be used as a reference guide for accident victims and their family members who have no idea what to do next.

After the initial emergency room trip, most people are confused about what their next steps should be. They don't have prior experience with catastrophic injuries (fortunately), and nobody taught them how to deal with these issues in school. But once it happens they may need to learn a lot of new things about insurance claims, financial obligations, liens, medical conditions and injury law. Even for healthy people, that's a lot to handle all at once. For people who are already struggling with injuries, pain, financial strain and insurance company red tape, the situation can be overwhelming.

That's one thing I hope to fix with this book. I want this book to be a simple, accessible guidebook for people dealing with a serious injury. You won't find any "legalese" written here. I intend the book to be as easy to read as possible. Once you finish this book, I hope you come away with a better idea of what to expect throughout the aftermath of an accident, from follow-ups with your doctors up to the day you settle or resolve your case. I also want to leave you with more information about whether hiring a lawyer is right for you, because I know many cases do not need the assistance of an attorney.

My mission over the last 16 years has been to assist and educate the public about accident claims and how insurance companies resolve them. Another important reason I wrote this book is because I want to help protect accident victims from the financial threat posed by insurance companies. You may be thinking, "'Threat?' But haven't I paid my insurance company to take care of me after an accident? Shouldn't the company have my best interests at heart?" While I agree that it should, that doesn't necessarily mean it will. You may have had a positive experience with your insurance company before - in fact, I hope you did. But as you will read several times in this book, insurance companies are not on your side.

Like all businesses, insurance companies are motivated to make money. They make money when they collect your premiums. They also make money by settling claims for a fraction of what the claim may be worth (this is especially true with very expensive claims, which is why the most seriously injured people are at the greatest risk.)

That means they don't want to pay you any more money than they have to. Paying an accident victim less means the carrier earns more, which translates into bonuses for the insurance company executives and a higher stock price for shareholders.

Finally, I wrote this book to answer your questions. For over 16 years as a personal injury attorney, I have come to realize that clients come to me again and again with the same questions - questions about fault, their insurance claims and the risks and benefits of filing a lawsuit. This book is an attempt to answer most of the common questions I receive from clients and potential clients.

However, I'm not aware of any book that can answer every question. There are always exceptions to every situation, especially in the field of personal injury law. Every case is different, and it's only after my office hears about your case that we can give you the answers that will fit your personal situation. No book can build the same relationship that a face-to-face meeting can. That's why I encourage you to contact us at The Davis Law Group for more information or if you have questions, suggestions or concerns.

DAVIS LAW GROUP, P.S.
2101 Fourth Avenue, Suite 1030
Seattle, WA 98121
Phone: 206-727-4000
Fax: 206-727-4001
DavisLawGroupSeattle.com

Introduction

In 2007, I wrote and published my first book for accident victims, "The Ten Biggest Mistakes that Can Wreck Your Washington Accident Case." That book proved to be an enormous success. We now receive nearly 500 requests per month for this book from accident victims and their families all over the state of Washington. Since that time I've gone on to write and publish several more books, some of which include "Long Haul To Justice: The Accident Victim's Guide To Semi-Truck Injury Claims," "When the Dog Bites: The Essential Guide to Dog Bite Claims," "Right of Way: The Essential Guide to Pedestrian Accident Law," and "Little Kids, Big Accidents: What Every Parent Should Know." All of these books were written to fulfill my mission and personal promise to educate the public about accident injury claims and how insurance companies handle them.

Despite the popularity of my books, I still felt there was a need to educate the public about the general field of personal injury law. My new book, "Washington Injury Law: A Reference Guide for Accident Victims," is more of an A to Z guide about the claims process and how personal injury cases are handled. This book is also the product of my first effort to collaborate with other personal injury attorneys and firms across the country to make sure the book is thorough and complete. I am quite happy with the final version, and I hope you will be too.

As you may now realize, we at the Davis Law Group are dedicated to helping accident victims recover fair compensation for their injuries. That's not just an empty platitude—it's our sole reason for existing. Our firm only handles cases on behalf of seriously injured people seeking compensation from the people and institutions responsible for their injuries. I am proud to say that we've helped hundreds if not thousands of clients over the past 20+ years to recover the money they need to pay their medical bills, support their families and make up for the injuries and permanent disabilities caused by another party's negligence.

About Davis Law Group

Davis Law Group was founded in 1994 with the mission of helping accident and malpractice victims and their families to get their lives back following a traumatic loss. Davis Law Group is a small, boutique personal injury law practice with an emphasis on representing a small number of clients so that each case receives individualized attention. A smaller caseload allows me and my staff to achieve superb results for our clients. The staff at Davis Law Group is also committed to serving each client in a manner that shows how important his or her case is to the firm, and how valued they are as clients. Rest assured I have hired only the most dedicated and committed personal injury legal staff to assist me in my mission of helping accident victims.

I have been a licensed attorney in good standing in the state of Washington since 1993. I have tried countless personal injury and wrongful death cases to verdict and I have successfully handled and resolved hundreds of accident claims, many of which involve auto accidents, wrongful death, medical malpractice, dog bite attacks, and other catastrophic injury cases.

I have been humbled by the awards and recognition that I have garnered throughout my years as a leading personal injury attorney in Seattle and throughout Washington state. Since 2006, I have been recognized as a "Rising Star Attorney" and a "Super Lawyer" 10 consecutive years by the legal publication Washington Law & Politics. I have also been listed by WLP in 'Who's

Who in Personal Injury Law' (The top 40 PI attorneys in Washington). In 2007, I was appointed to the Board of Governors of the Washington State Association of Justice. Since 2007, I've been recognized each year as a lawyer who is considered to be in the "Top 100 Trial Lawyers in Washington State" as determined by the American Trial Lawyers Association (ATLA). And in 2016, my firm – Davis Law Group, P.S. – was named the "Best Personal Injury Law Firm" in all of Washington state.

My skills and expertise as a trial lawyer have also garnered a good deal of local and national media attention. I have shared my legal commentary on various legal cases in the national media, including CNN with Anderson Cooper, The Huffington Post, and Inside Edition. Some of the cases handled by Davis Law Group are often featured on local news channels and programming, including KOMO 4 News, King 5 TV, KIRO 7 News, and QFOX 13 News.

In addition to representing accident victims, I have felt a professional obligation to help educate the public about the insurance claims process and those laws that impact the victims my office represents. As a result, I've authored several books and articles that help people understand their rights and remedies. This information has been hugely popular. At least two of my books have received media attention from various local news channels.

I also feel it is important to remain active in the community. That's why Davis Law Group has offered a number of scholarship programs to students in Washington state and throughout the country.

You can learn more about me and the Davis Law Group by visiting our website at DavisLawGroupSeattle. com.

How Davis Law Group Can Help

Because we work with injured people every day, we understand very well how devastating an accident can be. Our clients come to us with all types of serious injuries, from broken bones to chronic pain to brain damage and paralysis, as well as the wrongful death of loved ones. In every case we take, these injuries were the result of someone else's carelessness. Some of our clients will have to live with these injuries for the rest of their lives. In addition to the physical pain, the emotional trauma, shock and just plain unfairness of this situation are often emotionally very difficult.

On top of all this, our clients and their families typically begin to have serious financial problems as time goes on. In a serious injury, medical bills can easily add up to six figures, a sum that can bankrupt ordinary Americans. (In fact, one recent study found that medical bills are the most frequently cited cause of individual bankruptcy.) Hospitals will usually hold the injured person responsible for paying those bills, which means that victims and their families can be financially crushed if an insurance company refuses to do its job. Accident victims cannot work to earn that money, and their loved ones are likely to lose income taking care of them. And that does not even count other costs, such as a wrecked car.

As a boutique personal injury law firm, our goal and our job is to help solve this problem for injured people. A personal injury lawsuit cannot undo an accident, although we wish it could. But it can help victims pay the astronomical financial costs accidents cause, without devastating them financially as well. It can also compensate them for their injuries, physical pain and emotional suffering. In the best cases, it can even prevent the same accidents from happening to others, by penalizing wrongdoers and raising community awareness of the dangers.

Some people are uncomfortable with the thought of asking for money to compensate them for injuries. They believe—correctly—that no amount of money will reverse an injury or bring back a loved one. That's true, but unfortunately, science hasn't found a way to do those things. Instead, our civil justice system (and justice systems going all the way back to Biblical times) uses money as a way to penalize wrongdoers and make their victims whole, as much as possible. It may be a flawed system, but we do not believe anyone should be ashamed of using it for its intended purpose, especially if they are suffering financially because of the accident. And we have yet to meet a single client who would not give back all the money, in a heartbeat, if it could erase their injuries.

The justice system allocates money to accident victims based on their damages—that is, the injuries and losses they have suffered as a result of the other person's wrongdoing. You'll read more about this in Chapter Two, but you should know for now that your damages can be roughly divided into two categories: Economic damages, for financial costs related to the accident, and non-economic damages, for intangible but very real losses like the loss of a loved one's care and comfort. To collect money for those damages, you will usually have to prove to a jury that you suffered them. If the jury decides you have incurred damages, it then decides how much money is appropriate for each claim you make. Under some very extreme circumstances, you could be awarded damages of just one dollar.

All of this brings us to an important point: Suing does not mean you will get an easy windfall. If Davis Law Group takes your case, it means we think you have a strong claim, but no reputable lawyer will ever guarantee specific results. And even if you do get good results, it will probably take time and effort. But we can promise that we will work our very hardest to get you the best possible financial settlement or verdict—and we have a strong record of past successes that we would be proud to share with you.

All of this is possible because of the type of fee we charge—a contingency fee. Like almost all reputable personal injury firms, we never charge a fee at the beginning of the case. Instead, we are paid with a percentage of the money we recover for you—if you win the case. The percentage changes depending on the type of case and when it settles, but it will always be explained to you before you agree to hire us. If you lose, we will not ask for any legal fees at all. It's that simple. This allows us to represent everyone who comes to us with a strong case, regardless of their income or background.

This book is dedicated to explaining the nuances of personal injury and insurance law. One of the more common situations in which these principles apply is an automobile accident. However, my firm handles a wide variety of cases arising from all types of serious accidents, including:

Animal Bites	Motorcycle Accidents
Auto Accidents	Nursing Home Abuse
Bicycle Accidents	Nursing Home Neglect
Inadequate Security	Medication Errors
Defective Products	Construction Accidents
Head and Brain Injuries	Medical Negligence
Catastrophic Injuries	Wrongful Death
Spinal Cord Injuries	Quadriplegic Cases
Insurance Claims	Paraplegic Cases
Bad Faith Claims	Semi-Truck Accidents

Beware of Insurance Companies

As I have said many times before, insurance companies are not your friends. They may not actively wish you any harm, but make no mistake—their primary goal in the claims process is to save money by avoiding paying you any more than necessary.

When insurance claims adjusters begin working on your claim, they will crunch the numbers and come up with a range of values that they believe could adequately compensate you. Typically, they will then make you an offer from the low end of that range (or sometimes well below the low end of that range!). You do not have to accept this. Most people don't realize this, but they have every right to negotiate if they believe the offer is too low. Insurance companies rely on their customers' politeness, fear of bargaining or inexperience with bargaining and ignorance of their rights to keep them from negotiating. In the best-case scenario, you could reach an acceptable agreement with the insurance company without getting a lawyer involved.

However, victims of serious injuries are unlikely to be in the best-case scenario, because serious injuries tend to be very expensive. That means that accident victims need to be on the lookout for insurance companies' tricks and pressure tactics. After a serious accident, representatives from insurance companies have been known to contact accident victims within hours, days or weeks to discuss a settlement. They might offer victims a small amount of money; ask them to sign or record something; or pressure them to settle right away, before they have time to learn the full extent of their injuries.

This can have serious consequences down the road, because if you take a financial settlement from an insurance company, your claim is considered closed. If your doctor later says you need more medical care than you thought, you can't go back to the insurer and get more money. That's why we strongly recommend that clients wait a period of time before settling. If you feel at all pressured or suspicious, it's best to politely decline the insurance company's calls until you can speak to us or another injury law firm about your rights.

In one particular case, I met with a man whose life was forever changed due to the injuries he suffered after being rear-ended by a tractor-trailer. I recall a specific moment during the initial consultation where he mentioned that one of the trucking companies' lawyers asked him to sign off on a $5,000 check that the lawyer claimed would help him out while he was in the hospital, almost as if it was an act of good will on behalf of the trucking company. I began to grow concerned, and I asked him to show me the check. Sure enough, the man signed and cashed the check, which effectively meant that he had accepted a $5,000 settlement for the entire claim. Having already been victimized by the truck driver's negligence, this man also fell victim to the trucking company's high-pressure settlement tactics. Lying in the hospital bed in immense pain and worrying about the future, he was likely seen as an easy target. If only he'd had someone on his side, with his legal rights and financial future in mind, I can't help but think he would have experienced a much different outcome.

In the worst cases, insurers have been known to simply deny expensive claims that should be covered under the victim's insurance policy. They may use technicalities or half-truths, or simply accuse you of lying about how the accident happened. When this is done intentionally, it is called insurance bad faith, and it is illegal. If you believe you are a victim of insurance bad faith, you may wish to speak to us to learn more about your rights.

Featured Case Results

At Davis Law Group we handle many different types of accident cases. No lawyer can ever guarantee a specific outcome, nor represent that past results are an indicator of what we may accomplish in your case. But here is a list of past cases that we have successfully handled.

Traumatic Brain Injury	**$5,000,000 Settlement**
Wrongful Death – Auto Accident	**$4,000,000 Settlement**
Wrongful Death – Auto Accident	**$3,400,000 Settlement** *During Jury Trial*
Wrongful Death – Commercial Vehicle Accident	**$3,000,000 Settlement**
Traumatic Brain Injury Caused by Drunk Driver	**$2,150,000 Settlement** *During Jury Trial*
Serious Injuries in Semi-Truck Crash	**$2,000,000 Settlement**
Traumatic Brain Injury Resulting from Crash	**$2,000,000 Settlement**
Wrongful Death—Auto Accident	**$1,085,000 Settlement** *(total policy limits)*
Medical Negligence—Burn Injury	**$600,000 Settlement**
Nursing Home Negligence	**$500,000 Settlement**
Auto Accident—Herniated Disc	**$500,000 Jury Verdict**

In addition, we have settled and taken to trial thousands of smaller cases involving nonsurgical and surgical treatment valued below $500,000. Please remember that these are only a small sampling of the types of cases and successful results we have achieved for our clients.

Your Next Step

I wrote this book to provide a valuable resource for people who suddenly find themselves dealing with the difficult physical, emotional and financial fallout from a serious accident. I hope it gives you a good grounding in personal injury law, even if you don't end up filing a lawsuit.

Nonetheless, I know that no book can answer everyone's questions. Every case is different, and every client will have questions that can only be answered after we learn more about that person's unique situation. That's why I would like to invite you to come in and talk to us more about your case. We offer free, confidential initial consultations to those individuals who meet our case selection criteria—meetings where we discuss your case and its prospects. If you're not able to travel right now, we can usually bring this meeting to you, whether that means your home or a hospital bedside.

At a consultation, you can tell us exactly what happened and show us any documentation you might have saved. Then, we can give you our professional opinion about your case and its prospects should you decide to pursue a legal claim. However, this consultation is also a job interview of sorts—your chance to interview us. Please don't be afraid to ask us, or any other law firm, questions about our past results or other things that might be important to you. We know hiring a lawyer is an important decision, and we want to be chosen for our merits.

If you want to set up a consultation—or just have questions, comments or concerns—we encourage you to contact us.

Davis Law Group, P.S.
2101 Fourth Avenue, Suite 1030
Seattle, WA 98121
Phone: 206-727-4000
Fax: 206-727-4001
www.DavisLawGroupSeattle.com

Chapter One: Insurance

Even people who have never been in a serious accident often dislike dealing with insurance companies. If you have been in an accident and have a large or complicated claim to make, you may soon find out why. Unfortunately, talking to insurance companies is an essential part of recovering from your accident, and how you handle these interactions can make or break your case. In this chapter, I have tried to present some of the basic information you need to make your insurance claims as successful as possible — even when the insurer causes problems.

Are You Covered?

After an accident, one of your first concerns will probably be whether your injuries and property damage are covered by auto insurance. Luckily, you probably have at least some insurance coverage, because 48 states make auto insurance mandatory. (The other two, Wisconsin and New Hampshire, allow residents to drive without insurance as long as they have the financial resources to pay for any damage they cause in an accident.) Unfortunately, having some auto insurance is not the same as having enough auto insurance — and some drivers break the law by carrying none at all. This is bad news if you rely on the other driver's insurance policy to cover your injuries.

You should understand how insurance works in Washington State. There are two types of auto insurance systems in the United States, and which one you use usually depends on where you live. Most states are at-fault or tort states. This means the at-fault driver is legally responsible for any injuries and financial costs caused by the accident. The other driver's insurance policy is supposed to pay those costs, but you may have to sue the other driver to get payment if the facts are in dispute.

In Washington we also have no-fault auto insurance coverage. If your insurance policy has coverage called Personal Injury Protection (PIP), your own insurance company is required to pay for certain damages (like medical bills and lost wages) regardless of who's at fault for the accident. This is important coverage because it requires your carrier to pay for these expenses when they are due. However, this coverage is limited by the terms of your insurance policy. Most people who have PIP will have coverage of at least $10,000, but some may have the maximum of $35,000 (as of the date of this writing). Also, most PIP policies will only pay up to 85% of your lost wages starting two weeks after the accident. You should read your policy carefully to understand what other limitations and/or restrictions may apply. If you have questions you should speak to an experienced personal injury lawyer.

Contacting Your Insurance Company

After you receive medical care and recover from the immediate effects of your accident, one of the first things you should do is call your insurance company. You will probably also have to call the other driver's insurance company and let them know that an accident has occurred and a claim will be pursued. You should make that call as soon as you reasonably can, because waiting too long might make it look to the insurance company like you are exaggerating your injuries. Calling quickly is also part of your obligations under the contract you signed with your insurer.

This first call should be fairly short. Its purpose is only to give the insurance adjuster the basic facts about your accident and the information for the other driver's insurance company, if there is one. In fact, during the call, the insurance adjuster on the other end should never ask to record you or ask you to sign anything, especially in exchange for money. If you get this kind of request, you may be dealing with a dishonest company; you should politely decline and call a lawyer as soon as possible.

During your initial call, the insurance adjuster will probably ask you who was at fault for the accident or who was to blame. She might also ask if anyone got a ticket. If this is disputed or you truly are not sure, just stick with the facts. During this or any other conversation with an insurer, it is important to avoid apologizing or accepting blame just to be polite, because that could be taken as an admission of guilt. Also, if you were knocked unconscious or taken to the hospital, you may not have gotten the full story. One way to get it is to obtain a copy of the accident report made by the police (if one exists). If they will not release it, your insurance adjuster can get it for you and use it to start your claim.

Understanding Insurance Law Can Make The Difference

Often, a more detailed understanding of insurance law can make a big difference in receiving full compensation for your injuries. Take, for example, the case of a 25-year-old day laborer who was seriously injured as a passenger on his way to the beach with a few of his friends. His injuries were severe and permanent, rendering him unable to work anymore. The other driver was clearly at fault, since he rear-ended the vehicle the young man was riding in. That driver's liability insurance carrier said there was a total of $25,000 on his policy, so the young man would not be able to recover any more compensation for his significant injuries.

The young man consulted several lawyers who declined his case, saying there was limited coverage (the $25,000) and his bills already exceeded $100,000. Then the young man spoke to a friend who referred him to an experienced personal injury lawyer. That lawyer determined that while the vehicle the young man was riding in did not have underinsured motorist coverage, the trailer it was pulling did have coverage though his friend's father, a small business owner with a commercial insurance policy. The lawyer was convinced that there was underinsured motorist coverage through this policy, allowing his client to collect the full amount of his injuries.

The lawyer negotiated and "worked" the case for over a year, finally convincing the insurance carrier that this client could collect on $1 million in additional insurance coverage.

The lawyer was able to settle the case for the limits of the trailer's commercial policy and structure this additional settlement in a special needs trust, which allowed the young man to keep receiving Medicaid and still buy a specially equipped house and car. By fully investigating the case and understanding insurance law, the lawyer was able to fully compensate the young man and provide for his future medical and financial needs.

How Do You Get Your Medical Bills Paid?

If you received any sort of medical treatment after the accident, you will have to worry about medical bills and health insurance claims as well as auto insurance claims. Auto insurance should cover your medical treatment, but hospitals prefer not to wait to work out who was at fault. If you were not able to give them your health insurance information (if any) when you arrived, they will probably try to bill you personally. You or your lawyer should be able to get the bill sent to the appropriate party later.

If you have both medical and auto insurance, you may be wondering which will pay for your medical costs. In Washington, the hospital will start by billing you personally or billing the medical insurance company whose information you provide. Later, after you make your auto insurance claim, you or your health insurer may be reimbursed by the other driver's auto insurer. If you are among the few drivers who have medical payment coverage on your auto insurance policy, your own insurance company may reimburse you.

If you have no-fault insurance (PIP coverage), your auto insurance company should pay. The hospital may bill you personally at first, especially if you could not provide them with insurance information when you arrived, but it should be simple to transfer the obligation to your insurer. You may still have a deductible under your PIP policy. If your bills are higher than the amount of PIP coverage you have, any medical insurance will take over after your auto insurance coverage is used up.

If there are problems, keep in mind that in Washington you (the patient) are ultimately responsible for your own medical bills, regardless of whether some insurance policy should cover it. That means you should take action quickly if the insurance company refuses to meet its obligations.

Auto Repairs and Other Property Damage

If you were injured in your accident, the chances are good that there was also damage to your property. Damage to your car, truck or other vehicle is the most common type of property damage, but any other property you lost or had to repair because of the accident should also qualify. The same auto insurance policy that covers your injuries should also cover all of your property damage.

Generally, claims of damage to your vehicle fall into two categories. If the insurance company says your car or truck is "totaled," it means the repair costs are likely to be greater than the actual fair market value of the vehicle. That makes it not worth repairing, at least to the insurance company. (You are free to do what you like with a "totaled" vehicle.) The fair market value of the vehicle is determined by its age, condition, mileage, appearance, depreciation and other factors. Each insurer does this differently, and some take into account incidental costs like storage.

Because car loans and other financial obligations related to the vehicle are not considered in determining fair market value, your car or truck might be considered worth less than the amount you owe for it. This is especially likely with newer vehicles, which depreciate (lose value) quickly within their first few years of use. The insurance company is obligated to pay only the fair market value of the vehicle immediately prior to the accident, not the cost of repairs you made or your original purchase price. A special type of insurance called "gap insurance" is designed for this situation; it pays the difference between fair market value and any loans you still owe. Gap insurance is optional, but insurers often try to sell it to owners of new vehicles.

If the insurance company considers the vehicle repairable, it should pay for repairs by a body shop or a mechanic. Your insurance coverage may pay for your use of a rental car during repairs, or compensate you for the temporary loss of your car or truck. The carrier's obligation to pay for a rental vehicle will depend on the coverage of your own policy. If a rental car is covered by the other driver's carrier, then they are obligated to pay for a rental vehicle for a reasonable amount of time.

A reasonable amount of time for using a rental vehicle will of course vary according to the unique facts of each case. In Washington, you are free to choose your own repair shop. If you disagree with the insurance company's estimation of the damage, you can sometimes get a second opinion from another repair shop.

One frequent question we receive is whether your own insurance company or the at-fault driver's carrier should pay for the damage to your vehicle. Many times the at-fault carrier will promptly pay for the repairs and that should be sufficient. But other times, especially if there's a dispute about who caused the accident, your own insurance company will be forced to pay. It may also be advantageous for you to ask your own carrier to pay for the damage because in Washington there are special rules and regulations that require a person's own insurance company to act quickly. Those same rules and regulations usually do not apply to the other person's insurance company.

Dealing With Uninsured and Underinsured Drivers

If you were in an accident with an uninsured or underinsured driver, you may have an especially difficult task ahead. An uninsured driver is a driver with no insurance coverage at all; an underinsured driver is one with some coverage, but not enough to cover the damage he or she has caused. (A hit-and-run driver is considered an uninsured motorist, at least until he or she can be identified.) In Washington, your own PIP coverage may cover at least some of your injuries and property damage. But getting hit by an uninsured or underinsured driver may mean there is no money at all to cover your injuries.

You are free to sue, of course, but most uninsured or underinsured individuals are not wealthy enough to fully pay for a serious injury. Furthermore, it costs a lot of money to sue, just in expenses alone. Therefore, it may not be advisable to incur substantial expense when there is a low probability of collecting on a judgment obtained in a lawsuit.

Insurance May Cover You, Even With an Uninsured Driver

If you were hit by a driver without insurance, you may think you are out of luck — unable to collect any settlement at all. But before you give up, you should always call an experienced personal injury lawyer. An experienced personal injury lawyer is sure to look at all possibilities for insurance coverage, including insurance covering the driver, the vehicle's owner, and any user given permission to use the vehicle, as well as a client's own insurance coverage, before giving up.

In one case, Davis Law Group was able to help a distraught woman who was hit by an uninsured driver, causing severe injuries that required surgery. This driver was clearly at fault for the accident. In fact, he said at the scene that he knew he was at fault, but had no insurance to pay for the damage. The client had purchased collision coverage only, thinking she was doing the smart thing by saving money. Because neither driver had any insurance that applied to the crash, this woman thought she was out of luck. Still, she called us and we agreed to investigate further.

After investigating the facts, we discovered that the at-fault driver was driving his girlfriend's mother's vehicle—with the permission of his girlfriend in order to run an errand. Also, as it turned out, the mother and daughter had an agreement that the daughter could borrow her mother's car as needed from time to time. That meant the at-fault driver was a "permissive user" under the policy—someone who has permission to drive the car—which meant that he was covered by the mother's liability insurance.

This scenario is actually quite common. Although laws in every state require all drivers to have liability insurance, many violate the law. An experienced personal injury lawyer may be able to help by searching thoroughly for an applicable insurance policy covering any party involved in the accident. In this case it meant the at-fault driver was a "permissive user" under the policy—the daughter had permission to drive the car—which meant that she was covered by the mother's liability insurance.

In most states, liability coverage will cover permissive users of an insured automobile. This is true even though the driver of both vehicles involved in the accident were personally uninsured.

We at Davis Law Group always advise people to carry as much uninsured/underinsured (UM/UIM) coverage as they can afford, and preferably with limits of at least $250,000. This type of coverage supplements your basic auto policy. In fact, UM/UIM coverage is required to be offered to you by the insurance company in the same limits as your basic liability policy unless you reject the coverage in writing. UM/UIM coverage compensates you for the costs of the accident, up to the limits of the uninsured/underinsured policy. UIM coverage is a floating layer of coverage, which means it is added on top of the at-fault driver's coverage amount as an additional layer of coverage should you need it. Unfortunately, the actual cost of your injuries can still exceed those limits. And because uninsured/underinsured motorist claims can be difficult to document, some insurance companies make them difficult to collect.

Some accident victims make the mistake of believing that by pursuing a claim for UM/UIM benefits with their own insurance company the process will be much easier and less time-consuming. This belief is often unfounded. Even if you've been a loyal paying customer for 25 years and have never made a prior claim, your own insurance carrier may still vigorously contest or defend your claim. This is especially more likely to occur if your injuries are severe, thereby putting a large amount of money at stake in the claim.

When a Disability Takes You Out of Work

If your injuries take you out of work for more than a few days, you stand to lose a lot of income. If you have short-term or long-term disability coverage (under auto insurance or separately), you should be able to collect payments that help you make ends meet while you are out of work. If you are eligible for this coverage and decide to use it, you may hear from your insurance company about "subrogation," which is a legal term for transferring the obligation to pay from one party to another. (You can find more about subrogation in Chapter Six.) In Washington, the right of subrogation gives your disability insurer the right to be reimbursed if you recover any money for lost wages from a third party, such as the insurance company for the other driver. Because this issue can be complex, your lawyer should handle it for you.

You may be entitled to payment of lost wages from your own PIP carrier. Because you do not necessarily need to sue, subrogation is limited in certain circumstances. There may be certain defenses you have against paying a subrogation claim. Again, your lawyer should handle this claim for you to make sure you take advantage of all rights, defenses and remedies afforded under the law.

Dealing With Workers' Compensation Insurance

If you were at work during your accident, you are probably entitled to workers' compensation benefits. Workers' compensation pays the cost of any injuries you sustain at work and a limited replacement wage while you are unable to work, regardless of who was at fault for the injury. Your employer carries workers' compensation insurance to cover those payments. In exchange for collecting them, you agree not to sue your employer, even if you believe your employer caused the accident. However, if a third party was responsible for the injury, you may still be able to sue that party while collecting workers' compensation benefits. Subrogation may also come into play with a workers' compensation case, because multiple insurance companies are often involved in a claim.

Workers' compensation law is a complicated area that depends on its own set of laws and rules. Many lawyers focus their practice on this area of the law exclusively. Many workers have trouble collecting workers' compensation because replacement wages can be expensive — and insurance companies prefer not to pay expensive claims, even when they are legally obligated to. If you have a workers' compensation claim as a result of your accident, your lawyer may refer that part of your case to another lawyer who specializes in workers' compensation law.

Settling Your Claim with the Insurance Adjuster

Sometimes, it is possible to settle an accident claim by just working with the insurance adjuster. This is most likely when you have no injuries, or small or insignificant injuries that don't require a lot of medical treatment. In this situation, you may not even need help from a lawyer. However, before you close your claim you should make sure you have identified all of your injuries and property damage. You should not settle until you feel that you will be fully and completely compensated by the payments you will receive.

Many people do not realize that they are not required to accept the first settlement offer received from the insurance company. In fact, you are allowed to negotiate for the fullest compensation you are entitled to, using documentation from police, repair shops and other independent parties to support your claim. However, if your insurer refuses to change its offer then a lawyer can drastically change your situation. Hiring a lawyer to handle the negotiations lets the insurer know that you know your rights and are prepared to enforce them, if necessary.

The Adjuster Is Not Your Friend

Because we refer to "our" insurance companies, many people mistakenly believe that insurance adjusters are here to help us. Unfortunately, that is just not true. Insurance companies are in business to make money, and premiums — the monthly or yearly payments we make to have insurance — are just part of their profit. Like any other business, insurers make more money if they keep costs low. In an insurance company's case, that means paying less to people with expensive claims. The job of an insurance adjuster is to save the company money by settling your claim for as little money as possible.

Many clients have told me that they believed their own insurance company would do the right thing because these clients have good relationships with the insurance agent who sold them the policy. But the agent is often not employed by the insurance company and instead acts as an independent business owner. The insurance company's claims department acts much differently than the agent that sold you the policy. The job of the claims person is to minimize or avoid the obligation to pay you an amount of money. The claims person does not care how long you have been a paying customer of the company. They usually don't care that you've never had an accident nor filed a claim in the last 25 years. It all comes down to dollars and cents. If the claims adjuster can settle your case for 50 cents on the dollar, he or she is trained and instructed to do this for the benefit of the company. It doesn't matter what you think is "fair" or "reasonable", it only matters to the company how little it has to pay.

If you were seriously injured in your accident, you may not be in the best position to fight with your insurance company. Hiring a lawyer may be the best decision you can make to protect yourself, your family and your future.

Chapter Two: Understanding Your Injuries And Damages

In personal injury law, the wrongdoer (sometimes known as a tortfeasor) is responsible for all of the injuries caused by his or her negligence, or by any other unlawful conduct. If you are injured as a result of that conduct, you are entitled to full compensation for the injuries and damages that you have sustained. In the law, the goal is to make the injured party whole. That is, the purpose of monetary compensation is to try to restore you and your family to the position that you were in before the accident.

Once it is clear that the wrongdoer is at fault for the accident, an experienced personal injury lawyer can help you fully identify and understand your injuries. Your law firm will obtain and review your medical records and talk with you, your family and even your physicians to fully understand your injuries and how they have affected your life. Using prior experience with similar cases, your lawyer will then be able to predict the range of dollar amounts a jury might award.

In recent years, insurance companies, their lobbyists and big corporations have put forth a great deal of propaganda that casts personal injury victims and their lawyers in an unfavorable light. They do this purposely to bias potential jurors against personal injury victims and in favor of the people and insurance companies they sue. Often, the media exacerbates this problem by highlighting bizarre or rare multi-million-dollar cases. This creates the mistaken perception that most people pursuing personal injury claims receive unjust windfalls, or do not entirely deserve the compensation they receive. Nothing is further from the truth. In reality, most people injured by careless wrongdoers are hardworking Americans who just happened to be in the wrong place at the wrong time.

Proving Your Injuries Can Prove Your Claim

Sometimes, understanding your injuries can actually help prove your case. Take the case of a young boy who was hit by a car while riding his bike. The driver of the car claimed that she was not at fault and that the boy had simply run into the side of the car. Even the investigating police officer took the driver's word and decided the little boy was at fault. There were no other witnesses.

However, thanks to an experienced personal injury lawyer the boy's family had consulted, that was not the end of the investigation. The lawyer investigated and researched the particular type of leg fracture the boy had. To make a long story short, the lawyer was able to prove – using medical and scientific evidence – that the only way the injury could have occurred was if the car had hit the boy, as opposed to the boy running into the car. By fully understanding the injuries in the case, the lawyer was able to turn a claim denied by the insurance company into a substantial recovery to provide for the boy's future.

Follow Through With Your Medical Treatment

The full extent of your injuries may not be obvious immediately after an accident. Some people may feel that they did not sustain a serious injury, only to discover weeks or months later that what they initially thought was a minor injury has worsened and may require significant medical treatment. Because of this possibility, one of the things you should do after an accident is see a doctor for a full evaluation. Depending on the type of injury, it may be best to consult with a specialist. Be certain to tell your doctor about all of your symptoms, no matter how minor they may seem. You should see this doctor as soon as possible after your accident, so the doctor can properly document the full extent of your injuries. This documentation is important because it creates a clear record of your injuries and treatment, which is essential in a legal claim.

Immediately after the accident, it may be difficult even for the most experienced doctor to tell you how long you will require medical treatment. Depending on your injuries, you may need follow-up care for the first few weeks or months after you leave the hospital. For extremely serious injuries, you may need long-term or even lifelong care. Because it is often difficult to predict your needs early in a case, it is important for you to be vigilant about your health. If you notice a change in your symptoms, you should be certain to tell your doctor about it. You should also, of course, actively participate in your own recovery by following your doctor's orders, taking your medications and undergoing whatever rehabilitation or treatment your doctor recommends.

Your lawyer will also need to know about changes in your condition and how they affect your life, so he can explain the full extent of your injuries and damages to the insurance company and ask for the fairest settlement of your claim. To help your lawyer, you should keep a written record of your medical treatment and how your life has been affected by your injuries. This will also help you refresh your memory later, in case your claim goes to trial months or years after the accident.

When your treatment is completed or your doctor feels you have reached maximum medical improvement, your lawyer may request additional medical records, to better understand how the injuries will affect you in the future.

Medical Records Can Be Essential

Here's an example of a case where understanding the injuries was crucial. A 55-year-old carpenter received back injuries in a motor vehicle collision. The carpenter had been employed in the construction industry for 30 years at the time of his accident, and had back pain on and off throughout his working life due to the nature of his job. But he was always able to recover from whatever was causing his back pain and return to work without restrictions.

In this case however the carpenter's injuries from the car crash were persistent and never fully resolved, even after surgery. The at-fault driver's insurance company argued the injured carpenter's back problems were preexisting, so the car accident was not responsible for the injury. However, after a thorough investigation, the carpenter's lawyer was able to prove that the back injuries following the car crash were new and caused by that accident. The lawyer used medical evidence such as a detailed comparison of imaging studies taken before and after the accident, consultation with medical experts and further medical testing, to prove when the injuries occurred. This proof made the difference in the case, allowing the carpenter to recover a fair settlement to help with future medical care, his pain and other damages.

Different Types of Injuries

Under the law, a personal injury is any harm that you as an individual sustain, including physical injuries, financial costs and emotional trauma. Injuries can also be personal losses, such as losing the care and companionship of a loved one.

As you work to resolve your accident claim, you may hear insurance adjusters, lawyers and doctors talk about different degrees of injuries. You may hear injuries described as minor, moderate, severe or catastrophic. Minor or moderate injuries can be injuries such as sprains, strains, fractures, bruising or superficial cuts. These may be painful, but they usually heal well and quickly, with minimal medical treatment.

You may hear insurance adjusters refer to "soft tissue injuries." Soft tissue injuries are injuries to the non-bony parts of the body, such as internal organs, nerves, muscles and connective tissues. Sprains, whiplash and pulled muscles are all types of soft tissue injuries. Even if you have a bruise over the affected area, you and your doctor may not realize you have a soft tissue injury under the bruise, because it can be hidden from sight and hard to detect with tests. Soft tissue injuries may heal quickly, but some do not. Some can even result in chronic pain and disability, which can be permanent if not treated properly. Typically, it is harder to recover substantial compensation in these cases than in cases involving serious or catastrophic injuries.

A catastrophic injury is a serious injury that is expected to permanently change the victim's life. Examples of this type of injury include burns, amputations, spinal cord injuries, paralysis and head injuries (also called traumatic brain injuries). These types of injuries result in the most significant settlements and verdicts, because the injuries can be proven objectively and are more obvious to the insurance company or a jury.

Although catastrophic injuries are obvious in most cases, sometimes the full extent of the injury is not immediately revealed. This is especially true when the victim has suffered a traumatic brain injury, also called a closed head injury. In some cases, the brain may be affected in ways so subtle that only people close to the victim notice changes in abilities, behavior or personality. A closed head injury can be caused by physical trauma (a hard blow or penetrating wound), a blast wave from an explosion or violent shaking of the head. It often results from actual jostling of the brain. Such trauma can damage the tissues of the brain, which in turn affects the abilities controlled by the damaged tissue.

A concussion is the mildest form of a brain injury, but more serious brain injuries leave their victims permanently disabled. As one often expects, a brain injury may affect many aspects of the injured person's life, including physical movement, the senses, intellectual ability, creativity and even personality. Sometimes, what appears to be a minor concussion or brief loss of consciousness following a car accident can turn into in a more serious closed head injury later on, with symptoms such as chronic headaches, memory loss, loss of concentration or changes in a person's personality or behavior.

Permanent and Partial Disability

Unfortunately, some people's injuries lead to permanent disabilities, either partial or total. A permanent disability is any loss of ability that will affect the rest of the victim's life, and at least partially impair his or her ability to work or perform other day-to-day activities.

A permanent disability is often a major, life-changing event for victims and their families. In addition to the disability itself, disabled accident victims also face a higher risk of medical complications than uninjured people and often suffer profound emotional injuries because of their disabilities. People with permanent disabilities may require significant medical help, such as home health care nurses, extensive inpatient medical care and rehabilitation or long-term accommodation in an assisted living facility. Someone who has suffered a permanent disability is much more likely to recover a large judgment than someone who has fully recovered.

Medical Expenses

As everyone who lives in a modern society knows, health care can be very expensive. Even if you have medical insurance or good medical coverage through an auto insurance policy, you may be charged thousands or tens of thousands of dollars for a lengthy hospital stay, a trip to a specialized care center or repeated doctor visits and physical therapy appointments. If you do not have medical insurance, these costs can quickly add up and often exceed five or six figures in a short period of time. For someone who has suffered a catastrophic injury or a permanent disability, lifelong medical treatment can cost millions of dollars.

In a personal injury claim, these medical expenses are part of the damages (financial compensation) that you are entitled to claim. This is not limited to direct health care costs, but may extend to any medical expense, including prescriptions, medical devices and the cost of transportation to and from your doctor's office. Recovering your medical expenses is an essential element of your personal injury claim.

If your case involves a catastrophic injury, your lawyer will want to not only determine your existing medical costs, but also hire medical experts to determine the likely cost of your future medical treatment. In some cases, your law firm may need to hire an expert to develop a "life care plan" that predicts all of your future medical needs. This expert will evaluate your injuries, review your medical records and project the cost of future medical care.

Lost Income and Loss of Earning Capacity

If you are unable to work because of your injuries, you are entitled to claim the income you lose. In addition, if you have a disability that affects your future earning potential, you are also entitled to recover monetary damages for loss of the income you would otherwise have earned.

For example, let us say that you can no longer do the specific job you had at the time of the accident, but you find a job within your physical limitations that pays less than your previous job. In this case, you would be entitled to recover not only the income you lost from the old job, but also any future income you lose because you had to take the lower-paying job. If you are self-employed and your injury makes you unable to do your job, you may need to hire someone to replace you. You may be entitled to compensation for the extra money you pay to that person during your recovery.

In addition to your lost income and loss of future earning capacity, you may be entitled to recover any loss of benefits, such as health insurance, pension plans, bonuses or other benefits directly associated with your employment. An experienced personal injury lawyer will help you determine all of your financial losses so you can seek compensation for those losses. Your lawyer may need to hire experts, such as a vocational expert (an expert in work) or an economist. These experts will review your financial and medical records, then calculate and estimate the economic losses you have suffered from the accident. If you are self-employed, you can prove your economic losses through tax returns and other financial documents.

Pain and Suffering Damages

Another part of your personal injury claim is the way your injuries affect your daily life—your pain and suffering. Personal injury victims are entitled to recover damages for past and present suffering as well as any suffering they may experience in the future. These damages for pain and suffering are different types of damages from those you would claim for your economic losses or physical injuries. For example, someone who suffers chronic pain after an injury is entitled to be compensated for that pain and suffering.

Pain and suffering are not the same. Physical pain is a sensation and suffering is a mood. Pain is the awareness, through a stimulus in the brain, or something that could damage your tissues and is followed by a feeling of discomfort or unpleasantness. By contrast, suffering is an emotion that could be considered the opposite of happiness or enjoyment, and involves cognitive aware-ness of an unpleasant situation, or a lack of the pleasure the victim could have expected had it not been for the accident. Suffering could involve many emotions, including depression, anxiety and humiliation. For example, suffering could be embarrassment and anxiety from a disfiguring facial injury, an amputation, incontinence, paralysis or another injury that severely limits the victim's life activities.

Your lawyer's job is to help you prove how your injuries have affected your life and your family. The ultimate goal of a personal injury claim is to obtain the maximum possible compensation, so you may return to your life as it was before the accident. Although injuries make that impossible in some cases, you are entitled to seek compensation for every injury you suffer. An experienced personal injury lawyer will help you obtain the fullest and fairest compensation permitted by the law.

Loss of Consortium

In Washington, the law allows the spouse of an injured person to recover damages as well, even if the spouse was not injured. This is called a loss of consortium claim.

Black's Law Dictionary defines "consortium" as the "conjugal fellowship of husband and wife, and the right of each to the company, society, and cooperation, affection and aid of the other in every conjugal relation." Loss of consortium includes not only material services that you may lose because of a spouse's injury, but such intangibles as society, guidance, companionship and sexual relations. Usually, you may only make a loss of consortium claim when one spouse has been seriously injured, and that injury has had a direct negative effect on the marital relationship. You cannot make a loss of consortium claim if you are not married or just living with the injured person. A marital relationship is essential to making a loss of consortium claim.

Often, the non-injured spouse, at the direction of an experienced personal injury lawyer, can present compelling testimony at trial. This helps show a jury that the accident has affected not only the marital relationship, but also the family. Juries can sometimes empathize with the spouse who was not injured and better appreciate how the injuries have affected the marriage and other family members. An experienced personal injury lawyer can help you determine whether you should add a loss of consortium claim to your personal injury claim.

Common Defenses Used by Insurance Companies

At Davis Law Group we have years of experience dealing with the misrepresentations, exaggerations and outright lies insurance companies commonly use after injury victims make a legal claim. One common defense is to suggest that the victim suffered from similar injuries before the accident, or that the victim was predisposed to the type of injury he or she suffered. Yet another defense is to try to prove that the victim's injuries were not caused by the accident, but by other events in the victim's life (e.g., a prior fall, prior accident, or some other medical condition). When insurance companies cannot dispute fault for the accident they may resort to the age-old tactic of attacking the accident victim's character or preexisting medical history.

A good lawyer will successfully challenge these common defenses and help the victim present his or her injuries clearly, concisely and coherently. For example, even if you suffered from a similar medical problem (such as a back or neck condition) before the accident, your lawyer can help you prove that your previous injury was made worse as a result of your accident. Washington law supports the premise that a wrongdoer "takes his victim as he finds him." This means victims are entitled to recover full compensation even if they were particularly susceptible to an injury, or predisposed to experience greater pain or suffering than could have been foreseen by the defendant.

For example, you have a bad back that never required surgery, but then you are involved in a serious car accident that aggravates the back condition enough to require surgery, you are entitled to recover compensation for the surgery. After all, you would not have needed it if the accident had never happened.

Doctors and Other Medical Providers

If you have been seriously injured for the first time, you may be encountering types of doctors that you have never heard of before. The following are some of the medical specialists that personal injury victims are most likely to encounter.

An **anesthesiologist** administers drugs to provide pain relief during surgery. Some anesthesiologists also treat chronic pain. Anesthesiologists who treat pain are also sometimes called specialists in pain management.

A **burn specialist** is exactly what it sounds like — someone who cares for patients with severe burns.

A **dermatologist** handles diseases and injuries to the skin, including burns.

A **doctor of emergency medicine** usually works in an emergency room. This doctor may have been the first doctor to treat you after the accident.

The doctor you most likely see regularly is probably a **family practice** or **general practice doctor**. Depending on your injuries, he or she might take an active part in your care or refer you to a specialist.

Another common type of doctor is the **physiatrist** or **doctor of physical medicine and rehabilitation**. This type of doctor specializes in the non-surgical treatment and rehabilitation of various musculoskeletal conditions and injuries. A physiatrist or rehab doctor is often very good at describing and explaining your injuries and any limitations, impairment or disability that may flow from them.

A **neurologist** treats injuries and abnormalities of the nervous system, which includes the brain and spinal cord. This is the doctor you will see if you have a brain or spinal injury. If you need surgery, you might also see a **neurological surgeon** or **spinal surgeon**.

An **orthopedic doctor** or **orthopedist** treats injuries to the bones, muscles and joints, sometimes including amputations as well as broken bones.

A doctor who treats problems with joints is a **rheumatologist**.

For accident victims, **doctors of plastic surgery**, **reconstructive surgery** or **cosmetic surgery** work to correct damage to the body or unsightly scars, and to restore functions or prevent loss of functions.

Physical therapists and **doctors of physical medicine and rehabilitation** work with injury victims to restore movement or function to areas affected by an injury. This sometimes includes functions that you might not think of as physical, like brushing your teeth or writing.

Psychiatrists handle mental health issues, including emotional injuries caused by accidents. A psychiatrist is a licensed medical doctor who may legally prescribed medication.

Specialists in other specific parts of the body include **nephrologists** (kidneys), **hepatologists** (liver), **gastroenterologists** (the digestive system), **cardiologists** (heart), **pulmonary specialists** (lungs) and **podiatrists** (feet and ankles).

Common Medical Tests

If you sustained any sort of internal injury, including an injury to the spine, brain or internal organs, your doctor may ask you to take one of these special tests. This is good, because the more information you have about your injuries, the easier it will be to begin healing. This will also make it easier for your lawyer to prove your injuries. Tests you might take include:

X-rays are the radiation tests we are all familiar with; you have probably taken one at the dentist if you had your wisdom teeth removed. They show bony structures, so they are best for diagnosing bone injuries and cannot be used to diagnose soft tissue injuries.

A **CT scan**, sometimes known as a **CAT scan**, is short for "computerized tomography scan." A CT scan uses multiple x-rays taken in a circle around the same point to build a better picture than one x-ray could provide alone, using a computer to combine them. A CT scan is likely to be ordered if the doctors believe you have an injury to the internal organs of your torso or abdomen, or multiple fractures to a hand or foot.

An **MRI scan** is short for magnetic resonance imaging. The MRI is better for seeing soft tissues like muscles, ligaments, tendons, spinal discs, brain matter, and other tissues in the body. If you get an MRI, the doctors will ask you to lie down in a large tube that uses harmless magnetic radiation to look at soft tissues of the body. Sometimes they will also ask you to drink or have an injection of a substance that makes those tissues easier to see—called a contrast MRI. If your doctor suspects an injury to your brain or spinal cord, you might be asked to do this test. Because this technology uses magnets, you cannot use it if you have a pacemaker or other metal implanted in your body.

A **PET scan** is often used in tandem with a CT scan. In a PET scan, the patient is injected with a harmless substance that can be seen by the scanner using radioactivity. Unlike CT scans, PET scans can show your body's metabolic activity rather than just structures of the body. The images they produce are also three-dimensional.

If you know anyone who has had a baby recently, you are probably familiar with an **ultrasound**. An ultrasound test uses high-frequency sound waves that bounce off internal structures of the body to build an image. The image it builds is not as detailed as images from other methods, but because it does not use radiation, it may be the best choice for people with certain conditions. It is also less expensive than an MRI. Doctors use it to look at internal organs, connective tissue, bones, blood vessels and eyes.

A **discogram study** is a test to determine the anatomical source of low back pain. In this test, the discographer inserts a needle into the low back, or more accurately into the center of one of the lumbar discs. A radiographic dye is injected into the disc while the discographer views the procedure on a fluoroscopic video. If the injection reproduces the patient's pain, then typically it is believed that the particular disc is the source of the problem. This is usually a painful procedure.

A **neurotomy** or **radiofrequency rhizotomy (RF)** is a test where the physician inserts a needle into the facet joints of the patient's spine (typically in the cervical region). The test is used to treat chronic neck or back pain. The needle or wand is heated to a very high temperature by radiofrequency. The hot needle is then used to burn the nerves surrounding the joint to eliminate pain. This procedure is not considered permanent. The nerves will typically grow back, usually within 6 to 12 months.

If your doctors believe you have a nerve injury, you may take a **nerve conduction velocity study (NCV)**, an electrical test that can detect problems with your nerves. In this test, one electrode is placed over the nerve being tested, while another is placed in a "downstream" area of the nervous system. The speed it takes for the electricity to travel between them determines whether there is nerve damage.

An **electromyograph (EMG)** shows muscles' activity by measuring the electrical current they produce when they are in motion. This might be used for people with nerve damage, muscle weakness or the conditions that might cause them. In an EMG, a doctor inserts a thin needle into the muscle being tested or places an electrode over the area, then measures the electrical impulses of the muscle.

An **electroencephalogram (EEG)** is a test that measures and records the electrical activity of your brain. Special sensors (electrodes) are attached to your head and hooked by wires to a computer. The computer records your brain's electrical activity on the screen or on paper as wavy lines. Certain conditions, such as seizures, can be seen by the changes in the normal pattern of the brain's electrical activity.

An **endoscopy** uses a flexible tube with a light and a camera to look inside natural openings in your body, such as the throat. This is most commonly associated with tests on the stomach or colon, but can be used in any area with a natural opening.

Health Care Facilities

If you are seriously injured, you may end up at a health care facility more specialized than the hospitals we are all used to. If you need this kind of care, you might even be transferred from your original hospital to one of these facilities:

A **trauma center** handles patients who have sustained a sudden and serious physical injury. They are ranked from Level I to Level IV, with the most serious cases at Level I facilities. Because they are expensive to run, they are not common; patients outside major cities may have to be airlifted to one. In Washington, the only Level I trauma center is Harborview Medical Center in Seattle.

A **rehabilitation center** is a facility where patients work to reestablish or relearn abilities they lost because of a serious injury, through therapy. Physical therapy helps with movement or prevents loss of movement, while occupational therapy might focus on relearning activities of daily life or finding ways to perform them despite a new disability.

Burn centers focus on patients with serious burns. They not only treat burn injuries, but work to help patients return to everyday life, often with therapists, social workers, psychiatrists and other professionals who are not conventional doctors.

Assisted living facilities may be appropriate for injury victims who need long-term physical or occupational therapy and help with everyday living. This might be true of someone with a severe brain injury or spinal damage. In addition to providing meals and housekeeping, as at a nursing home, the staff at an assisted living facility works with patients to help them regain independence and abilities. Some patients are able to return home eventually; others may need to remain in a facility throughout their lives.

Home care is an option for patients whose injuries do not require full-time hospitalization. A nurse or other health care professional might visit every day or a few times a week. Depending on the injuries, the professional might do anything from changing bandages to administering a treatment with an IV to helping with personal needs.

Chapter Three: Choosing A Lawyer

The lawyer you choose may be one of the most important factors in determining the success or failure of your case. Such a decision should be made with care. Unfortunately, choosing a lawyer can be intimidating for people who have never been through the claims process. You may be justifiably concerned about ending up with a lawyer with bad ethics or poor skills. In this chapter, we hope to ease those fears and provide a basic guide to finding a personal injury lawyer.

The first thing to consider is that lawyers, much like doctors, often concentrate their practices in a specific area of the law. If you need hip replacement surgery, you probably want to see an orthopedic surgeon, not a cardiologist. You may also want that surgeon to routinely perform hip surgery on other patients instead of doing the procedure a few times per year. Similarly, if you are in an accident, you will not want to hire a lawyer who focuses on divorce or real estate or business law. You probably don't want a lawyer who does a few personal injury cases a month or year, along with other types of cases. Although a non-specialist lawyer may be able to help you, he or she will likely not have the same experience and skills that a lawyer who specializes in personal injury law day in and day out. No one person can do it all. The same is true for lawyers who specialize in a particular practice area. A lawyer who specializes in personal injury law will likely understand the individual nuances in the legal, procedural and evidentiary areas that come with representing accident victims. They will also better understand and implement the successful strategies that can maximize the value of your personal injury claim, because they work with these issues every day.

At Davis Law Group, we find that many of our clients come to us after a recommendation from someone they know who has hired us in the past. For this reason, you may want to begin the search by talking to family and friends. Ask if anyone can refer you to a personal injury lawyer who helped them get good results, or who they have heard good things about.

You can also do your own research to find a lawyer. The internet is a good place to start. Some very reputable personal injury lawyers provide substantial information on personal injury claims and the law on their websites. Sometimes the lawyer's successful cases are reported in the press and may show up on news feeds or in newspaper stories. Sometimes the lawyer may be featured on news stations or other programs as a credible source the media turns to for information about personal injury matters. If that's true, that lawyer may be a good choice.

More and more lawyers are using video on the internet. This may be a good source to check out a lawyer. Look for a lawyer who actually offers helpful information about the type of case or injury you may have. Stay away from those lawyers who only brag how good they are, or how successful they have been in the past. Although success is certainly important for obvious reasons, the lawyer's video should do more than just brag; it should actually help the potential client understand his or her rights or some potential problem that often arises in personal injury cases.

Many reputable personal injury lawyers and law firms in the Greater Seattle area – myself included – use TV advertising to reach new potential clients. Although this may be a good place to start your search for a lawyer, I would not rely solely on TV advertising to make your decision. Any lawyer who advertises or promises a quick settlement of your case likely does not have your best interests at heart, as the successful resolution of a case often requires a tremendous amount of work. Also, many lawyers rely on companies who run the advertisements for them – these companies allow any paying lawyer to be first on the referral list, and these attorneys may not necessarily be the most ethical or qualified to handle your specific case. Be careful.

Top Ten Myths of Personal Injury Lawyers

There are many myths about personal injury lawyers. Here are what I consider to be the Top Ten Myths:

Myth #1   All personal injury lawyers have basically the same training and experience.

Myth #2   Any lawyer that graduates from law school can try a personal injury case in court.

Myth #3   All personal injury lawyers go to trial at some point.

Myth #4   A personal injury lawyer that never goes to trial can get just as good settlements as one who does go to trial.

Myth #5   A lawyer who is "good at DUI cases" or "real estate law" will also be able to effectively handle personal injury cases.

Myth #6   A "lawyer referral" service is always a good way to find the right lawyer for your case.

Myth #7   The bar association determines whether a lawyer can advertise that he is a "personal injury specialist."

Myth #8   The personal injury lawyer who appears in advertisements will actually be the lawyer who handles your case.

Myth #9   An attorney who advertises or promises a "quick settlement" will always have your best interests at heart.

Myth #10   A law firm with dozens of offices throughout the country has more experienced lawyers than a smaller firm.

Choose Your Lawyer Carefully

Here's a sad story about a lawyer who advertised on T.V. in Rochester, New York. The attorney, Jim Schapiro, ran aggressive T.V. commercials which promised to obtain large financial settlements for victims, referred to himself as "the meanest, nastiest S.O.B. in town," and claimed to have aggressive courtroom prowess. Schapiro, who called himself "The Hammer," had law offices in the states of New York and Florida.

In 2002, one of Schapiro's clients, Christopher Wagner, sued Schapiro for malpractice. Mr. Wagner had been injured in a car accident and had responded to one of Mr. Schapiro's television ads. Mr. Wagner alleged that he had incurred medical bills of $182,000 but that Schapiro's firm advised him to accept a settlement of only $65,000 from the driver and then promised that he could get more money by filing suit against the state of New York. It turned out that the state had no liability for the accident and Schapiro never pursued Mr. Wagner's case further.

In a video deposition, Jim Schapiro testified that he had never tried a personal injury case in court and that he had been living in Florida for the last seven years. Mr. Wagner's attorney also discovered that Schapiro's Rochester law firm staffed just one lawyer who had only tried 4 cases. A New York jury found that Schapiro had engaged in misleading and deceptive advertising and that he committed malpractice. Schapiro was ordered to pay $1.5 million to Wagner.

Consequently, in 2004 Schapiro was suspended for practicing law for one year by the State of New York. In 2005, Schapiro was then suspended from practicing law in Florida for one year. In 2004, four additional clients sued Schapiro alleging that he had engaged in misleading advertising and had committed malpractice. Thereafter Schapiro stopped practicing law and instead now writes books for injury victims.

Mr. Wagner's case is a reminder that one should carefully choose a lawyer who has good ethics and experience trying cases in court. The lawyer should also be a specialist by having a practice that is devoted to personal injury law.

Remember, all lawyers are not the same. The same is true for personal injury lawyers. Make sure you do your homework when it comes to choosing a lawyer. The decision you make can have good or bad consequences in your personal injury case.

Why Hire a Lawyer?

The question may enter your mind: Should I even hire a lawyer, as opposed to just dealing directly with the insurance company and its adjuster? You should know that although the insurance adjuster may seem friendly and cooperative, he or she works for the insurance company that will pay to settle your claim. If the insurance adjuster can persuade you to settle your claim for less than what it is worth, that is good for the insurance company but bad for you. Unlike a lawyer you hire, the insurance company has no legal duty or financial incentive to treat you fairly!

Case in point: A working-class mother had a serious accident with a commercial tractor-trailer rig. She was injured in the accident and her car was so badly damaged that it was useless, both of which posed challenges for this mother of three young children. The very next day, she was visited at home by a representative from the truck driver's insurance company. The insurance adjuster was very skilled at creating an expectation that he was there to help her deal with the problems the accident had caused. After learning that she had no medical insurance, he told her that he believed she would make a good recovery, based on his experience and the way she was able to get around in her home and carry one of her children. Based on this evaluation, he offered her cash to repair her damaged vehicle, and $1,000 to compensate her for the trouble and pain she may have experienced. All she needed to do was accept the cash that day and sign the release, barring her from making any further financial claim.

Although tempted, she called her husband at work. He told her not to accept or sign anything and to call a lawyer immediately.

After contacting a lawyer, she eventually found that she had severe injuries to her shoulder and would need a period of treatment and testing to see if she could recover without surgery. Fortunately, she recovered without surgery after receiving the necessary treatment, and was fairly and fully compensated for her months of suffering and damages. Ultimately, she received nearly 50 times what the adjuster wanted her to accept. As you can imagine, this client was immensely pleased with the decision to retain a lawyer rather than deal directly with the insurance company alone.

The Initial Consultation

When you first call a law firm, your call may be taken by a lawyer, a paralegal, a case manager or an intake specialist. This person will ask you for basic information about you, as well as the details of your accident. Based on your answers, a lawyer will make an initial assessment of your case and may schedule a consultation. If you cannot travel to the law firm, many personal injury lawyers are willing to have the consultation on the telephone, in your home or at the hospital. At our firm, we make every effort to accommodate clients and potential clients with this type of need.

During the initial consultation, you will be asked for details about your accident and your injuries. Because details can be hard to remember, and because some clients feel intimidated or stressed by this meeting, we recommend that clients bring all of the documents they have that are related to the accident — things like police reports, hospital bills, medical records, photographs, witness statements, your insurance policy and anything else that may be in your possession. Don't worry about not having enough information. Often times the lawyer will be able to request the documents or reports needed. We always do our best to put clients at ease and explain everything as thoroughly as possible, without "legalese."

Questions the lawyer is likely to ask at your consultation include:

1. Did anyone receive a ticket?
2. Was a police report made? If so, do you have a copy?
3. Did you take photos of the vehicle?
4. Did you take photos of your injuries?
5. Did you give a statement to police, insurance adjusters or anyone else?
6. Were there any witnesses, and if so, did anyone get their contact information?
7. How much damage was done to your vehicle? Do you have a repair estimate?
8. What medical treatment have you had thus far?
9. What medical treatment, tests or follow-up are currently recommended by your treating physician(s)?
10. How are you feeling?
11. How are your bills being paid?
12. What insurance companies are involved?

Once you have thoroughly discussed the case, the lawyer should discuss the method of calculating fees. Most reputable personal injury lawyers work on a contingency-fee basis. This means that the fee is a percentage of any recovery that the lawyer secures on your behalf. With a contingency fee you are not required to pay for legal services up front, or at all, unless and until the case has been won. The lawyer should have a fee agreement that specifies how the fee is calculated. The contingency fee can range from 25% to as high as 50%, or more if the case is complex and extremely risky. Sometimes the fee may vary depending on whether the claim is settled or tried in court. Most cases do not have to go to court. But if it does, there is often a substantial amount of extra work that goes into the case, and hence a higher fee may be justified.

This arrangement may sound strange, but it remains popular because it allows ordinary folks to hire the best lawyers to take on their case. Most people don't have the resources to pay a good lawyer $300 or $400 per hour. The contingency fee arrangement "levels the playing field" so to speak so someone with limited financial resources can still hire a good lawyer. The contingency fee arrangement is an essential and valuable part of our legal system, providing access to justice for everyone, no matter what their income or background might be.

What Is the Next Step?

When you find the right lawyer, you will sign a contract formally retaining this person as your lawyer, giving you all of the rights of a client. To get the case started, your lawyer may direct staffers to obtain your medical records, doctors' notes and medical test results, along with a copy of any police or accident report and any insurance information or statements the insurer might have recorded. If necessary, the lawyer might also retain a private investigator to find important but elusive information about your case. All of this case development takes time. At Davis Law Group, we have found that clients really appreciate being kept informed, whether or not we have anything significant to report. For that reason, we assign specific staffers to update clients regularly about the status of their cases.

In this first stage, your lawyer is working hard to understand the facts and the strength of your case. After the case is built, your lawyer can begin negotiating with the other side to get you the best possible compensation under the laws of your state and the facts of your individual case. You may end up settling the case outside of court or participating in a full trial. You will learn more about this process, the stages of a lawsuit and your own responsibilities in Chapters Four through Seven.

What if My Case Is Rejected?

Unfortunately, sometimes lawyers must turn down cases. In order for a lawyer to accept a case, he or she must consider many factors, including the severity of your injuries, which parties were at fault, conflicts of interests, legal limitations, time constraints and more. If the firm decides that it cannot handle this case for you, that may not necessarily mean that you do not have a case—just that this firm is not in a position to accept your case.

At Davis Law Group, turning down cases is one of our least favorite aspects of our work. When we have to tell clients that we cannot take their cases, we do our best to refer them to a local bar association or another lawyer who is better suited to help. We also try to provide them with educational materials, like this book, to help them better understand the system and where their cases may fit into it.

Chapter Four: You Have Become A Plaintiff—What Now?

You have been injured through someone else's conduct, and you know you may be entitled to recover financial damages. You have decided to hire a lawyer to represent you and bring a legal claim to recover those damages. You are now a plaintiff.

The most important thing for you to do now is focus on getting better. That means you need to follow your doctor's advice and keep all of your appointments. If your doctor prescribes physical therapy, tests or other medical procedures, you should follow through their recommendations. If your doctor writes you a prescription for medication to help you heal or manage pain, you should not delay having it filled.

Not only will this help you get better, but it also creates a paper trail that supports your personal injury lawsuit. Your doctors' records are very important in personal injury cases, as they are often the primary way your lawyer can prove the nature and extent of your injuries and symptoms. The records also act as medical testimony in your case and help determine the value of your claim. It is vital that you follow through with your doctors' recommendations; otherwise the insurance company's lawyers will use this to lower the value of your claim.

Keeping Diaries and Calendars

Your lawyer may ask you to keep a diary or calendar of your activities, focusing on your physical and psychological injuries. This may seem like a chore, but it can help your legal case because it helps prove the nature and extent of your injuries, your pain and how they affect your life. If you sustained serious injuries in the accident, your treatment may continue for months and your healing patterns may change over time. It may also be important to keep a record of the changes you notice, both positive and negative, starting soon as possible after the accident. In some cases, even your treating physician may benefit from your notes.

In your diary, you should focus on how you feel and how you are coping with your injuries. Make these entries as often as you feel a change; there is no need to make an entry every day. To begin, write down your name and a start date. On any day after the accident when you notice any changes in how you feel, or experience anything unusual, write it down. Include the date and a brief description of what you are feeling and what you were doing when you felt it. Include any descriptions of things that seem important, such as events that seem to trigger pain.

It is important not to forget the diary as time goes on. At the beginning, you may make daily entries, but as you start to feel better, you may find yourself making entries that are further and further apart. It is absolutely fine to make fewer entries if you have less to say, but it is important not to forget your diary altogether. Unfortunately, some injuries continue to have occasional side effects, even after they seem to have healed..

You should use the calendar to record each of your doctor's appointments or other medical care. When you record a diagnostic appointment, be sure to note the type of test, such as an MRI. It is better not use this calendar to record social appointments or chores that are not relevant to your case. However, you should also record the dates and times of appointments with your lawyer, and any deadlines or court dates he or she provides.

Your Diary Matters

Clients and potential clients frequently tell personal injury lawyers "I am not the suing type." Many people are injured by someone else's wrongful or negligent act, yet they are either afraid of filing suit or do not know what it takes to bring a claim. Essentially, bringing a claim means that you become a plaintiff. This may seem like a daunting task to many people. However, the simplest tasks assigned to plaintiffs can often have huge rewards.

In one case I know about, a client came looking for a lawyer nearly two years after the accident. He was severely injured in a car accident, causing his right arm to be paralyzed. He waited so long to get legal help because he assumed there was no one to collect from since the other driver left the scene and was never found. He did, however, keep a diary of his daily life over the two years since his accident. In it, he noted every time a nurse came to his house, every time his mother had to drive him to therapy and even how excruciating the pain was on a daily basis.

After investigating the case, his lawyer discovered that the client was entitled to uninsured motorist insurance under a policy issued to the client's employer. After a two-week trial, he was awarded a multimillion dollar verdict. The client's daily diary was very important because it helped explain to the jury how the accident had affected the client's life.

Pre-Litigation Settlement

Many clients are surprised to learn that they might be able to settle the case before they even file a lawsuit. In fact, most personal injury claims are settled without the need for a lawsuit, or very early on in the litigation. This is possible because the job of a personal injury lawyer is to negotiate with insurance companies. This includes both your own carrier and the company or companies for the other parties involved. A quicker settlement may be accomplished if there is little or no question that the other driver is at fault for causing the accident and your injuries. It may also happen when liability is still in question, but your injuries are very severe.

During the pre-litigation process, your lawyer verifies that the at-fault person has insurance coverage, and then determines whether your own insurance policy provides coverage for the accident. Your lawyer will also investigate the facts surrounding the accident, reviewing the police report, interviewing the witnesses and inspecting the scene of the accident in order to get the best possible information on how the accident occurred and who is at fault. The lawyer will also review your current and prior medical records in an effort to understand your claim and to prove that your injuries were caused by the accident and not some other preexisting medical condition.

After thoroughly investigating your claim, your lawyer may then begin to determine the value of the claim. There is no magic formula when it comes to evaluating personal injury claims. Generally speaking, a case is worth the amount of damages inflicted on the person who has been injured. These damages may be easy to calculate, like past and future medical charges, lost earnings, lost earning capacity, and property loss. But the law also states that the injured person has the right to recover compensation for other "intangible" harms. It is these "intangible" harms that are more difficult to calculate. Such harms may include those subjective harms that the person has experienced from the injury, including pain, agony, disability, loss of enjoyment, inconvenience, and mental anguish.

The intangible harms suffered by the accident victim are purely subjective, difficult to determine and often vary among the people (or jurors) who are deciding the case. Ultimately, the value of a case is determined by the jury (or a judge if no jury demand has been filed). Both sides—your attorney and the insurance company or defense lawyer—are continually trying to evaluate how a jury might see the case and how much money a jury might award. Then each side will assign a value or a value range, and try to negotiate a settlement close or above each side's own range.

Often times it may take many months or years before the value of a case can be adequately assessed. One reason for this is because of the slow progress of the person's recovery or rehabilitation. Another reason is due to the complexity of the injury or condition which may cause a significant delay in a firm diagnosis by the treating physician. In many instances a case should not be settled or resolved until the person obtains maximum improvement following the accident, and this can also contribute to the delay of achieving a reasonable resolution of the case.

In most cases the value of a claim is driven primarily by the extent and severity of the person's injuries. Other important factors to consider include the type, extent and frequency of past medical treatment and the need for future treatment. I also rely on several other factors to help me determine the case value. These factors may include, but are not limited to, the client's likeability as a witness and his or her credibility, the facts of the accident giving rise to the case, the extent and permanency of the injuries, the client's age, whether the client missed time from work, the identities of the at-fault insurance company and its defense attorney, specific legal or evidentiary issues involved in the case, the county or venue where the case has been or will be filed, and the amount of settlements and verdicts for similar types of cases that I and other lawyers have handled in the past.

You should note that no two cases are alike, even if the accident and/or injuries involved are nearly identical. This means that the evaluation of two cases which appear to be similar on the surface may actually produce widely different evaluations due to the other factors involved in the case. Evaluating personal injury cases takes a lot of knowledge, experience and some hard-earned intuition. Usually a lawyer that has experience trying cases in front of a jury develops a good understanding on how to evaluate the worth of any given claim. Without these traits you may be at a serious disadvantage when negotiating with the insurance adjuster. And unless you are in the business of evaluating and settling personal injury cases for a living, you should usually look to an experienced personal injury attorney for guidance.

Follow Your Doctor's Orders

Following your doctor's recommendations will help you make a full recovery. And it will also help your legal case. That was underscored by one trial involving a woman who was rear-ended by another driver while she was parked behind a bus.

After the crash, the woman was taken to the hospital with complaints of back and neck pain. After an examination including X-rays, the emergency room doctor instructed the woman to follow up with her medical doctor if she still had problems.

The next day, the woman still had back pain. She called her chiropractor and received treatment for her crash-related injuries. At trial, the defendant argued that the plaintiff did not follow her doctor's orders because she saw a chiropractor rather than a medical doctor.

The jury returned a lower than expected verdict for the woman because they believed the woman should have followed the ER doctor's instruction to see a medical doctor. In their view, the jury believed that a medical doctor might have saved some additional treatment expense by recommending alternative methods of treatment.

Pre-Litigation Mediation

Many times the parties will agree to participate in alternative dispute resolution (ADR) to resolve the case short of trial. One type of ADR is called mediation. The mediation may come at the suggestion of either the insurance adjuster or your own lawyer. Some of the superior courts in Washington actually require that the parties participate in mediation. Mediation entails the use of a "mediator" who assists the parties in reaching a settlement. The mediator is an impartial person who is paid by both sides to help them resolve the case. Mediation allows both sides to present and argue the relevant facts of the case and the extent of the costs and damages to the mediator who then will work to help them agree on a settlement. These independent mediators are often retired judges or people with special court certification, so they should have experience with the laws and issues that are important in your case. Mediation is a voluntary proceeding. That is, neither side is obligated to settle the case at mediation. (For more on mediation and other forms of alternative dispute resolution, see Chapter Six.)

If no settlement is reached at mediation, the case proceeds with litigation and ultimately a trial. The failure to settle at mediation will have no effect on your right to continue your case.

The Case Settles

If a settlement is reached, either through negotiation or pre-litigation mediation, the insurance company will send a check to your lawyer. They will also send legal documents, often called a "release" and "hold harmless" for your signature. By signing these papers, you relieve the insurance company and the at-fault party for your injuries of any further obligations or payments related to the injuries and damages from the accident. The hold harmless document obligates you to protect the carrier and the at-fault party from any liens or claims asserted against your settlement recovery. These are standard and customary documents that must be signed in a personal injury case. You must sign these papers as a condition to collecting the settlement proceeds.

Your personal injury lawyer should have a trust account. This account holds money belonging to others. The trust account obligates the lawyer to protect these funds on your behalf. Once the settlement check clears the trust account, your lawyer will prepare a settlement statement or closing statement for your review and signature. This is another legal document, which sets forth the total amount of the settlement and any deductions for fees, costs, medical bills, liens or other amounts that must be paid out of the settlement proceeds. You will have the opportunity to review this statement, and your signature will authorize your lawyer to send you your settlement funds. Once you receive the proceeds from the settlement, your case is successfully concluded. For more on settling and closing your case, please see Chapter Six.

Chapter Five: Litigation

Oftentimes, trying to negotiate a reasonable settlement with the insurance company is a waste of time. More and more insurance companies are taking a very aggressive stance in settling personal injury or accident claims. Certain carriers have a reputation for making unreasonably low settlement offers, even if the injuries are severe. Often times the insurance companies use pre-lawsuit negotiations to find out as much as possible about you, your lawyer and your doctors. This can result in unfair advantage to the insurance company not to mention a complete waste of time and effort. For these reasons, it may be advantageous to file a lawsuit immediately and then continue negotiating the claim if possible. Once a lawsuit is filed, the court will set certain deadlines including a trial date. These deadlines, and in particular a trial date, can help motivate the insurance company to make reasonable attempts to settle the case promptly.

Even though many claims are resolved before a lawsuit is formally filed, there may be additional reasons to file a lawsuit earlier than usual. If there's a question about whether insurance exists, or how much insurance exists, a lawsuit may be commenced early so the lawyer can use the discovery rules to find this information out. Sometimes the statute of limitations requires that a lawsuit be commenced immediately. This is the time limit that the law imposes to bring a claim. Other times it may be necessary to file suit immediately to preserve evidence and force the other party under subpoena to give a statement under oath or to turn over important evidence and information.

When Do You File Your Lawsuit?

The law of each state sets deadlines by which you must file your lawsuit. These are called statutes of limitations, and they are usually calculated either from the date of your injury or from the date you discovered an injury that was not immediately obvious. (They may also be extended for minors and people with certain disabilities.) For example, the statute of limitations for most personal injury lawsuits in the state of Washington is three (3) years. Statutes of limitations are different in each state and often change according to the type of case you have, but all of them are hard deadlines. That is, if you wait too long, you will not be able to pursue your case, no matter how strong it is. One of the first things your lawyer will do after learning about your case is calculate the statute of limitations that applies, and take any action necessary to preserve your right to sue.

There are also legal deadlines that apply in certain specific circumstances. For example, if you plan to sue a government agency, you may be required to give that agency notice within a relatively short period of time, or file an administrative complaint, before you may sue. In Washington, if a party wishes to sue a governmental entity he must first file a claim with that entity and then wait 60 days before filing the lawsuit. The failure to comply with this rule may mean the dismissal of your lawsuit. Because these deadlines can be short and missing them can take away your right to sue, it is essential to learn about them and take action as quickly as possible. This is one reason why personal injury lawyers prefer to see you as soon as is practical after your accident.

Filing a Lawsuit

Your lawyer's office should take care of the actual filing of the lawsuit in court. But in general, you will file your case in the county where your accident happened, or in the county where one or both of the parties involved lives, depending on the circumstances and the laws of your state. The county where the case is filed is sometimes called the "venue." In Washington, the case must usually be filed in the county where the claim or accident arose, or where the defendant resides or transacts business. Your lawyer can explain how these rules affect your case.

A lawsuit formally starts when you file a written complaint with the court. This complaint describes the facts of the case, your injuries and why the person you are suing is responsible for your injuries. It then separately lists each "cause of action," which is a reason for suing, and finishes with a request for financial compensation for the injuries you have listed. This can be quite detailed, depending on your state's requirements, but it always contains enough information to inform the other parties why they are being sued.

Along with the complaint, your lawyer will also file a summons, a document that must be personally served on the defendants. The summons explains how the defendant should respond to the complaint and gives a deadline to do so. As a courtesy, your lawyer may send a copy of the complaint to the defendant's insurance company.

After the complaint is filed, your lawyer may have to specify whether you prefer a jury trial or a "bench trial," in which a judge makes most of the decisions. You and your lawyer should have agreed on this ahead of time. In a jury trial, a group of randomly selected citizens from the area decides the case while the judge acts as a referee and resolves legal issues involved in the case. By contrast, a bench trial involves a judge deciding the entire case (issues of fact and legal issues). Bench trials are less common than jury trials. If your lawyer recommends one, he or she should be able to explain why.

Who Answers the Complaint?

After the complaint is filed and served, the defendant's insurance company will usually assign the matter internally to an employee called a litigation claims adjuster, who will oversee the claim. This person's job is to try to resolve your claim before trial, or handle the claim in a way that helps the insurer at trial. Insurance companies do not like to be sued, of course; they may take extra steps to resolve your claim after the lawsuit is filed, so you may be able to settle at this stage. However, for this chapter, we will assume that you will not settle right away.

The insurance company will also assign one of its own lawyers, or hire an outside lawyer, to represent the defendant in court. The first task for this lawyer is to prepare a document called an answer to the complaint. This document will either admit or deny the allegations contained in the complaint. The answer may even say that other parties are at fault for your injuries and should be added to the lawsuit. The answer may also set forth any defenses the defendant is planning to use in the case that explain why he or she is not responsible for your injuries.

If the defendant fails to answer the complaint or fails to file it in time, you can ask the court to simply declare the defendant in "default." A "default judgment" is not common and it can usually be set aside under specific circumstances.

Sometimes the court will immediately set a trial date when the complaint is filed. Other courts may require one of the parties to file a document which formally requests the clerk to set a trial date. It may take as long as two years or more to be called for trial. It really depends on the court where the action is filed. If the court is in a heavily populated region, or if the court receives a large number of filings, the trial can be scheduled on a date far into the future.

Discovery

Discovery is the process of exchanging information about the case with the other side of a lawsuit. This is a formal legal process governed by set rules. The law requires that both sides of a lawsuit share information about the case with one another on request. (Certain things, such as privileged communications between you and your lawyer, are exempt from discovery even if they are specifically requested.) In most cases, the information exchanged includes information about your accident, the injuries you sustained, the nature and cost of your health care, the effect of your injuries on your life and your family, your employment background and your educational background.

The discovery phase is extremely important because it permits both sides to learn about the facts and issues of the lawsuit before trial. This allows both sides to build a case and evaluate the strengths and weaknesses of their positions. During settlement talks, the information you receive during discovery can be invaluable.

Your Records Are Essential in Discovery

As a plaintiff, you now have the responsibility to prove your case. Legally the defendant does not have to prove anything. This is because the burden of proof is on the plaintiff; that is, the plaintiff must prove each and every element of the cause of action. Take the case of a 37-year-old construction worker who was hurt when a load of cement blocks were partially dropped on him, driving him to his knees. This injury caused debilitating back pain, and because of it, he was never able to return to work.

The problem in the case was that all of the damages were based on an invisible injury — pain. Pain is very difficult to prove. But in this case, the injured worker was extremely consistent about attending all of his medical appointments, kept very good records, established reliability with his medical providers and had a long-established reputation for honesty and hard work.

Because of this consistency and reliability, all of the witnesses in the case were willing and able to give favorable testimony. The injured man's medical providers were able to explain and support his claim for the unseen injuries. As a result, his lawyers were able to convince the defendants of the substantial risk of taking the case to trial, winning an out-of-court settlement large enough to supplement the man's lost income and provide security for his family. In his role as a plaintiff, the worker did his job successfully so that his lawyers could do theirs.

Interrogatories

Typically, the first step for both sides in discovery is to send written questions for the other side to answer. These written questions are called interrogatories, and in many areas, you will answer these questions under oath, even though they are written and you will not be in a courtroom. Interrogatories may consist of several written questions that ask you about the accident, your background and your damages, including any past injuries or problems for which you have sought health care, as well as any previous legal claims you were involved with. You may also be asked to provide details about any income you lost or information about your past employment. The goal is to build a story about the relevant parts of your life before and after the accident. When you have provided your answers, you will sign them and they will be sent to the defendant's lawyer.

We find that some clients are initially reluctant to answer these questions, because they can be personal or stray into topics considered impolite or irrelevant. Your lawyer can and will formally object to an inappropriate interrogatory, or to a number of interrogatories that exceeds limits set by court rule. However, these questions are usually being asked because they are relevant to your case. Most of the information about your health and your finances is considered "discoverable," which means it is a fair question during discovery. Your responses help the parties and your own lawyer learn the information they need to evaluate your claim.

Requests for Admissions

Another written discovery tool is called requests for admissions. This is a document that simply asks one side to admit or deny certain facts relevant to the case. If you dispute or deny a request for admissions, you must write down the facts that you believe support your position. Your lawyer should help you with this. Using requests for admissions helps both sides determine which facts are agreed upon, which are disputed and which must be part of the lawsuit.

It is important to respond to requests for admissions in a timely manner, because if you miss the specified deadline, the court may behave as if you admitted the truth of the matters asserted in the request.

Requests for Production

Requests for production of documents—that is, asking the other side to send copies of specific papers—are an important part of the discovery process. Requests for production may come with interrogatories, but both sides are free to request production of documents throughout discovery.

Requests for production should be requests for documents that are relevant to the lawsuit, the accident or your damages. This often includes copies of your health care records, receipts or invoices for your health care expenses, accident reports, witness statements and pictures of the scene of the accident. If you are claiming a loss of income, you will probably be asked to provide your tax returns for several years prior to the accident. You may even be asked to produce any notes or diaries you have kept. Either side may request any discoverable document. Your lawyer may review the request for production with you and help you copy the documents and send them to the defendant's lawyer. If your lawyer believes the request for a document is improper, usually an objection will be asserted. The objection may be resolved between the lawyers or the judge if no agreement is obtained.

In addition to requesting documents and evidence from you, the defendant's lawyer may also ask other people or parties for information. Most commonly, the defense attorney may request copies of your medical records directly from your treating healthcare providers. The defendant may also be entitled to request documents about you from your current and former employers, schools you have attended, and from the military if you have served. Additionally, if you have applied for Social Security benefits, the defendant's lawyer may request information about your claim from the Social Security Administration. You may feel uncomfortable with these requests, but if the information is discoverable, the defendant's lawyer is entitled to ask for these documents. In fact, you may even be required to sign forms authorizing release of the information.

The Importance of Being Earnest During Discovery

Complete disclosure of information during discovery is an important way to achieve a settlement. And it is also important if you end up in trial. This was illustrated by the case of a client who failed to inform her lawyer that she had been denied a promotion at work because of her injuries, resulting in over $20,000 a year in lost income. She thought it would be better to "surprise" the insurance company with this information later at trial.

However, because this client had failed to disclose this information during discovery the defendant was able to convince the judge to exclude it at trial. The defense attorney argued that he was surprised with this new information at trial and had no opportunity to prepare for it. The judge agreed. The client was prohibited from mentioning this important fact to the jury.

This mistake cost the client an amount of up to $400,000 over her lifetime for lost wages she attributed to the accident. Although the client still won her lawsuit, she could not recover additional compensation for her future lost income. This could have easily been prevented had the client been open and forthcoming with her lawyer and the other side.

Depositions

A deposition is a face-to-face meeting where the attorneys are allowed to ask a witness questions under oath while a court reporter transcribes the session. Any witness that may offer relevant information about the case at trial can be deposed, including you, your doctors, and your friends and family. Either side may request a deposition at any time, but the request is most likely to come after you have responded to interrogatories and requests for production of documents. If your deposition is requested, it is very important that you prepare for this with your attorney. Your conduct at the deposition can influence the value assigned to the case and also affect the likelihood of whether the case will settle before trial. A deposition is a little like an oral version of interrogatories.

Many of our clients are nervous before depositions, but that is quite common especially if it is your first deposition. There's no need to worry, however. Your lawyer will be there to observe throughout the deposition and can object to inappropriate questions or ask for breaks if you need them. This is important, because it is essential for you to stay calm and professional during a deposition. This is the first opportunity for the other side to evaluate you in person, so you should appear neat and as confident as possible. You should usually dress neatly and conservatively so you make a good impression.

Your lawyer (or his or her staff) should prepare you ahead of time for the questions in your deposition. You may be asked to attend a meeting where you review all of the written information your lawyer has, as well as any responses you gave to interrogatories. It is especially important to make sure that your testimony is truthful and consistent with these interrogatory responses, because the lawyer for the defendant will probably question you closely about any inconsistencies. This process should also help refresh your memory about the details of your injuries, your treatment and your recovery.

At your deposition, you will probably start by reviewing the information in your written interrogatory responses. The deposition is an opportunity for the other side's lawyer to clarify or have you explain those written answers, and to obtain additional information. As we said, it is important to make sure that your testimony is truthful and consistent with your interrogatory responses, so the other lawyer does not spy a seeming inconsistency between your oral testimony and your written testimony. Your answers should be based on your own personal knowledge; do not guess. If you do not know or remember the answer to a question, you should say so. Many people feel embarrassed to admit they do not know something or had a memory lapse, but these things are only human. And when you are under oath, it is important to be as straightforward as possible.

As with the written discovery, you may feel that some of the questions are invasive or do not directly relate to your accident. However, unless your lawyer objects or tells you not to respond, you should answer every question in the most honest way you can. The court rules actually give wide latitude to the lawyer on what questions can be asked, or what areas can be covered. If some of the questions upset you, you can usually take a break during your deposition testimony, although you may have to respond to any unanswered questions first. If you would like a break, you can simply tell your lawyer. If the break is allowed, you will be permitted to get up, walk around, get a drink of water or just clear your head.

Discovery and Settlement

The discovery tools outlined in this chapter are only some of those available in a lawsuit. These tools represent the most common types of discovery performed in any given case. Although discovery may seem time-consuming, the process of exchanging information can actually help increase the chances that settlement will occur. And if the parties are still not able to resolve their case after discovery, the information they exchange during discovery will help them build evidence for their case and narrow the facts and issues that must be decided at trial.

Mandatory Arbitration

In Washington, most of the superior courts have adopted a program known as "mandatory arbitration." Arbitration is another way to resolve a case instead of going to trial. With arbitration, the court appoints an "arbitrator" who will decide the case by listening to testimony, reviewing evidence, and then issuing an award.

The arbitrator is usually an experienced attorney or retired judge.

The purpose of Mandatory Arbitration is to reduce court congestion, expedite the litigation process, and to provide a cost effective resolution of civil claims. Arbitration is often preferred over a jury trial because the costs are much lower, the rules of evidence are relaxed, and the hearing itself is far less stressful than a jury trial.

Also, the arbitration hearing may be scheduled within four to six months after a lawsuit is filed while it can take up to 2 years or more to get to trial. Most arbitration hearings last no longer than a day while a jury trial usually takes at least 3 to 5 days.

There are potential drawbacks with arbitration. For instance, there is a limit on the amount of damages that can be awarded. In Washington (as of the date of this writing) that limit is now $50,000. But even if your case is worth more than $50,000 it could still be advantageous to participate in mandatory arbitration due to the high costs and risks of going to trial. Another potential drawback is that either party can appeal the arbitration award and request that the case be tried in court. However, if a party appeals the award but fails to do better at trial, that party will have to pay the other side's attorney fees and costs (which could be substantial depending on the facts of the case and the length of trial).

In my experience, more than 90% of the arbitration appeals are requested by the defendant's insurance company. Most plaintiff attorneys do not like to appeal an arbitration award because it creates a significant risk that the client may have to pay the defendant's insurance defense costs if they get a worse result at trial. What most people fail to recognize is that many insurance companies will intentionally appeal a fair arbitration award to force the plaintiff to incur the substantial added expense of trying the case in court. They do this because these same insurance companies want to make it as expensive and time consuming as possible to wear down the plaintiff and his or her attorney. In fact, many insurance companies will routinely spend more money to defend a case than the amount of money it would take to simply pay the arbitration award.

If the arbitration award is appealed and the case goes to trial, the jury will never be informed that the case was submitted to arbitration. And of course, the jury will never be told the amount of the arbitrator's award. This can create problems especially in smaller cases because the jury may be left with the impression that the plaintiff and his or her attorney have forced the jury to come to court to decide a small case. Many times jurors resent having to decide a small case because they believe smaller cases should be settled. Yet jurors never realize until after the trial that it was the defendant's insurance company that appealed the award and forced a trial.

It is important to remember that there are specific rules that govern Mandatory Arbitration. These rules are complex and can provide traps to the inexperienced attorney. You should always consult with a qualified and experienced personal injury attorney about whether your accident case is appropriate for Mandatory Arbitration.

Chapter Six: Settlement

Statistically, most cases settle voluntarily, and without having to go to trial. Trials take time, are expensive and take a lot of work. They can also produce unexpected outcomes. From a personal perspective, an experienced personal injury lawyer may want to take a case to trial—but the decision to go to trial is always left to the client. The job of an experienced personal injury lawyer is to help clients achieve the best result in their case. We find that most of the time, the client wants the matter resolved quickly and fairly, so settlement is usually preferred. However, if a fair settlement cannot be reached the matter must be resolved by trial.

Experienced personal injury lawyers also understand that a settlement should not be rushed. Settling a case is often a process. Good settlements usually take time and effort. The process can be complex and take many months or even years. Different lawyers initiate the process in different ways (who goes first and so forth), but it always ends up with an offer and a series of counteroffers and counter-demands. However, the numbers passed back and forth are based on the many facts involved. A good lawyer will prepare the case for trial in an effort to get the best settlement possible. The settlement offers and counteroffers will be based on the evidence that each side expects to present and hear at trial. A party that has prepared a strong case for trial may be in a better negotiating position when it comes time to settle the case.

Deciding whether to accept a settlement offer requires you to consider subjective as well as objective factors. For example, there are benefits to ending your claim sooner rather than later. Litigating the case can take a high toll emotionally. On the other hand, the time, anxiety, energy and risk assumption required to go to trial may be worth it for the client—because of the potential for greater compensation. Client objectives vary, and each case and each client is different. The settlement process offers an opportunity for dialogue—and out of this dialogue will come a decision that fits the client in that case.

There are numerous factors to think about when considering a settlement offer, but issues to consider start with the amount of money being offered, the conditions attached to the offer and the amounts owed to third parties — like health care providers or other insurance companies. There are laws and contractual obligations that govern these third parties' rights to participate in the distribution of settlement proceeds. These rules are part of every settlement agreement, and you are expected to know them. An insurance company has no duty to explain the rules to you. Third parties such as health care providers might also claim part of your settlement behind the scenes.

What you and your law firm must determine is the true value of the offer being extended. That is, you need to know how much of the money offered will end up in your pocket. To answer this question, the lawyer has to solve the puzzle (so to speak) that is the totality of the client's claim, with the goal of maximizing the claim's value. An experienced personal injury lawyer will analyze these and other issues behind the scenes, so the client can focus on the challenge of recovering from injuries and putting his or her life back together.

The lawyer participates in settling cases—but it is always the client who makes the final decision. The lawyer's job is to prepare the client to make an informed decision. And, of course, the lawyer will provide the benefit of his education and experience. Emotions also play a role in the settlement process. However, your lawyer must remain as objective as possible to get the best result. You want a clear and level-headed attorney to guide you through the settlement process.

Sometimes the courtroom is the right place to resolve a case, as long as the client makes that decision after being informed of the risks, costs and potential benefits. Understand, however, that your lawyer will work to give you a realistic assessment of the benefits and risks associated with settlement and trial. That way, you can make an informed choice.

Understanding a Settlement Offer

First and foremost, you and your lawyer will discuss whether the amount of the offer is reasonable under the circumstances. Your lawyer should be able to give you a professional opinion on this, weighing the likely outcome of a trial against the certainty and benefits of settling now. Rejecting one settlement offer does not mean you will never get another. In fact, some defendants even expect to go through several rounds of offers and rejections.

A settlement offer is always measured against this one question: "What will a jury do in your case?" No one knows for sure of course. But the reasonableness of a settlement offer is whether a jury may award an amount close to the offer or some amount that is much higher or lower. If your lawyer believes it may be difficult to get a jury to award much higher than the offer, then the settlement offer should usually be accepted.

There is also a difference in the settlement value of a case versus the actual value a jury may decide. The settlement value of a case is always less than the actual value of a case. This is because the settlement value takes into account the enormous expense and risk of going to trial. The settlement value is always a judgment made by the parties. The settlement offer has to be high enough to persuade the claimant to accept the offer to avoid the increased risk and expense of going forward with litigation and a trial. For example, if there is a strong defense concerning liability (i.e., the defense can show that a jury might not find the defendant at fault for the accident or find that the plaintiff shares a good portion of the fault), then the settlement value of case will be reduced even further to reflect the risk that no fault or little fault may be assessed against the defendant. Insurance companies will always evaluate settlement value lower than what a jury verdict might be. Again, the insurance carrier knows that the plaintiff will incur risk and expense by going to trial so the offer will reflect these uncertainties.

Other considerations involve what debts, claims or other liens might exist against your settlement recovery (we will discuss and define liens in the next section). Your lawyer will try to get a settlement offer that will take care of any and all deductions that must come out of your settlement. If the settlement offer is not be sufficient to pay all of these debts, you may be liable for the rest. Sometimes, your lawyer can help by negotiating or using other remedies available under the law to make sure all of your obligations are covered. Depending on the circumstances, your lawyer might be able to convince creditors to take a lesser amount in exchange for immediate payment. But because this is an uncertain process, it is important to discuss your debts and obligations with your lawyer when analyzing a settlement offer.

At this stage, your lawyer may also talk to you about subrogation, which we discussed somewhat in Chapter One. A subrogation claim is a type of claim where another party has an interest in your settlement recovery. Often times a subrogation claim is asserted by your own health or auto insurance company or by another party that has advanced money for your injuries or damages. For example, if you have medical insurance, it probably covered your initial medical care. But if an auto insurance company is legally obligated to cover those costs, the medical insurer may be entitled to reimbursement from the auto insurer or from you, out of any settlement you reach with the auto insurer. Subrogation can be complex and may depend on state and federal laws as well as individual contracts. Your lawyer should help you understand how it applies to you.

If you have claims against more than one defendant or insurance company, or are considering a lawsuit over the same injuries against another party, you should also consider whether settling with one defendant could limit or eliminate your right to pursue the other claims. Washington follows the law of comparative negligence (also called comparative fault). This term means that more than one party may be responsible for a plaintiff's damages according to each party's percentage of negligence. For example, let's say Party A and Party B both negligently injured a person and that person's damages were calculated at $100,000. Party A was found 25% responsible and Party B 75%. Party A's share of the damages is $25,000 and Party B's share is $75,000. Under the law of comparative fault, each negligent party is only responsible for its share of damages as determined by the jury (or a judge if the matter is tried without a jury, i.e., bench trial). However, the law of joint and several liability may hold each defendant jointly responsible for the entire verdict and not just that defendant's proportionate share. But to obtain joint and several liability, you cannot settle with one defendant and go to trial against the other defendants. For this reason it may be prudent to settle with all defendants at the same time or go to trial against all of them.

Quick Settlement Recovery Helps Family in Need

Sometimes, a quick settlement is one of the most important services a personal injury lawyer can provide, as illustrated by a tragic wrongful death case. In this case, a young and growing family was in a serious car accident that killed the wife and her unborn child, leaving the husband a single parent of a two-year-old. Thankfully, the two-year-old was not seriously injured. The husband, his mother and his child filed a wrongful death lawsuit.

Because the driver responsible for the accident did not have substantial assets, the family's law firm knew it was important to identify and collect from all available insurance policies. The firm worked quickly and was able settle these claims in just eight months, for an amount exceeding $1 million. Although that money could never bring back their lost loved ones, the large settlement was recovered relatively quickly and allowed the surviving family members to move on with their lives.

How Liens May Affect Your Settlement

Liens are legal claims against your settlement recovery. The most common type of lien in a person injury claim is one asserted by your health or auto insurance company for medical treatment paid on your behalf. Another type of lien is one asserted by your healthcare provider. If the hospital or your doctor is owed money for your treatment following the accident, they can assert a lien in your settlement, or on your home or other property.

Resolving lien claims can be difficult because of the many complex laws that apply to them, and because holders of lien claims are often slow to respond in writing to questions about their liens. Unfortunately, the law does not always say that lien holders are required to respond to your lawyer within a specific time. Sometimes it takes months to get an appropriate answer. This delay prevents prompt payments of settlement funds to clients like you, and can be frustrating for you and your lawyer. Unfortunately, this time delay may be unavoidable depending on the type of lien and the identity of the lien holder. Your law firm should work hard to obtain this information and resolve these issues, so that the settlement can be distributed and you can resolve your case.

One example of a complex lien claim that may take some time to resolve is a Medicaid or Medicare lien. If Medicaid or Medicare has paid for some of your treatment they are entitled to reimbursement of those payments. These federal programs will then have a lien on your settlement. Your lawyer will probably have to hold back a part of your settlement equal to the debt until you can negotiate an agreement and pay the agency. Medicare and Medicaid are notoriously slow in responding to information about their liens, so delay is likely. Again, your settlement funds cannot be distributed until you reach an agreement and pay Medicare.

When multiple insurers or debts are involved, this can become quite complex. For example, you might run into complicated lien problems when you have your own private insurance (including a settlement from a personal injury case) but are using Medicare as a secondary insurer. When it is not certain whether Medicare is a primary or secondary insurer, Medicare will make a conditional payment. If it is later determined that some other party was responsible for that payment, Medicare is entitled to a refund from that party, or from you or the health care provider, if one of you was paid by that party. The federal government may place a lien on your property to recover this type of conditional payment.

Take Care with Medicare

Cases involving Medicare may be more complicated than cases involving private health insurance. One family using Medicare found this out after the mother was seriously hurt in a car accident. They were unable to resolve their claim with the wrongdoer's insurance company, so they hired an experienced personal injury lawyer. After the lawyer was able to settle the case for $300,000, the family thought the matter was resolved. However, they soon discovered that Medicare was demanding all of the settlement proceeds for reimbursement of the medical bills it had paid on the mother's behalf. In fact, Medicare wanted money for treatment provided to the mother before the accident.

Their experienced personal injury lawyer was able to distinguish the charges for treatment of the auto accident injuries from the other types of treatment. Medicare, because it is a government entity without any true controls, took months to review the case. After extensive negotiations with Medicare, the lawyer was able to substantially reduce Medicare's claim.

Another problematic lien is the ERISA lien, which stands for "The Employee Retirement Income Security Act of 1974." ERISA is a federal law that gives special rights to employers with respect to health care plans.

Typically the ERISA lien is much more onerous than your typical state law created lien. For instance, there are certain equitable defenses available to you when dealing with a state-law created health plan lien. This means that your attorney may be able to compromise or completely eliminate the state law lien, and thereby maximize your settlement recovery. Not so with the ERISA lien. Recent federal and Supreme Court decisions have taken many of these state law defenses away. Unfortunately, this means that you may have to pay back the ERISA plan 100% out of your recovery. Again, you should consult with your lawyer about the ERISA lien because there still may be certain defenses available so that the lien amount can be reduced or avoided entirely.

Ways to Reach a Settlement

In this book, we have referred a few times to "settlement negotiations." However, negotiating directly with the defendant's carrier and his lawyer is just one way you can reach a settlement. I previously discussed "alternative dispute resolution" which typically refers to mediation and arbitration. Both methods are ways to avoid trial and resolve the case.

Direct Negotiations

The most direct way to reach a settlement is simply to negotiate with the insurance adjuster, or the defendant and the defendant's lawyer. Doing this requires substantial knowledge in two areas: The prospects of your case if you go to trial and the value of your claim. This is where having a lawyer can provide immense benefit. Experienced personal injury lawyers have usually handled hundreds or even thousands of cases like yours, so they understand how your case is likely to come out at trial. They should also be familiar with the courts and juries in your area. They also know which evidence may be admissible or inadmissible in your case. For these reasons, they will be in the superior position to evaluate and resolve your claim for full value. And of course, a lawyer is an experienced negotiator. This levels the playing field against the insurance adjuster or defense lawyer, who will work to minimize your payments to save money for the insurance company.

Once you retain experienced counsel, he will handle all contact and negotiations with the insurance company and the defendant. Legally, the defendant and his carrier and lawyer can no longer contact you directly. Under most circumstances, you do not need to be present for direct settlement negotiations, although your lawyer will keep you informed throughout. Using the information you provided about your case and the information obtained during discovery, your lawyer will build the strongest possible case for settlement and present it to the other side. If they make an offer, your lawyer will present it to you for a decision, along with his or her advice.

Mediation

I discussed mediation previously in this book. To recap, mediation is a type of settlement negotiation in which an impartial third party helps both sides come to an agreement, using training in dispute resolution methods and legal experience. Mediation is usually conducted through an in-person discussion with all parties, including you, the insurance company and/or the defendant, as well as the lawyers for all parties. Generally speaking, a mediator is a retired judge, a lawyer or other neutral person who has also been trained to mediate disputes. Frequently, he or she has a special certification from the courts or the bar association of your state. However, unlike a judge, a mediator must be paid. Usually, you and the defendant will split this cost evenly. Mediation can be chosen or ordered by the court at any time during your case, although it is more likely after discovery has been conducted.

Your lawyer should be very skilled in mediation sessions. There is a process and routine that should be followed in these special sessions. Often times the mediation involves thought-out strategy regarding the negotiations. Your lawyer will want to have prepared thoroughly for the mediation and be ready to address arguments or weaknesses in the case presented by the other side.

Arbitration

We previously discussed arbitration. This is another form of alternative dispute resolution. Like mediation, it brings the parties together before an impartial third party who understands the applicable law and will keep order during discussions. And like mediators, arbitrators are often retired judges or lawyers with experience in the legal area affecting your case, with a fee that will usually be split evenly between the parties. But unlike a mediator, an arbitrator does not actively guide the conversation or give opinions. Arbitrators are more like judges who keep order and rule on questions about the law, and eventually, on which party should prevail.

Arbitration may be nonbinding or binding. With nonbinding arbitration, the resulting judgment is only a suggestion. In binding arbitration, the decision is final and non-appealable. Binding arbitration can be advantageous for parties who want to resolve the case more quickly, less expensively, and to obtain a final resolution. The identity and reputation of the arbitrator is extremely important, particularly in binding arbitration since the final decision may not be appealable (hence the term binding arbitration). Often times the arbitrator is agreed upon by both sides. Hopefully your experienced personal injury lawyer will be familiar and comfortable with the arbitrator so that your chances of a favorable outcome are increased.

Closing Your Case

Reaching a settlement can provide some satisfaction in knowing that your legal claim is finally going to be behind you. But you must still complete the closing process, which is an important part of finalizing your case and this can take time.

Usually, you will be asked to sign a release and hold harmless agreement that formally extinguishes all current and future claims against the at-fault party and/or insurance company for your injuries and damages. A hold harmless agreement protects the defendant and the carrier from any liens or claims made against the settlement recovery. Because signing these documents terminates your right to collect any more compensation for your injuries, you should understand them and go over them with your lawyer if you have questions.

As part of the closing process, your lawyer will have to pay out of your settlement proceeds any outstanding bills, claims or liens. Sometimes this process takes time so your lawyer may be forced to hold some or all of your proceeds in a trust account until everyone has been paid or until all claims or liens have been resolved.

The net settlement proceeds will be released to you after you sign a form called a closing or settlement statement, which typically ends your case and your client relationship with the law firm. It also lists all of the disbursements of the settlement funds, which includes payment of legal fees and costs, outstanding medical expenses, liens and any other debts to be paid out of the settlement, as well as your own payment. Again, you should not hesitate to bring up any questions or concerns about this document. If you have special circumstances or a particularly complicated case, your lawyer may bring up other ways your settlement proceeds might be disbursed, or have suggestions designed to serve your best financial and legal interests. Your lawyer cannot write you a settlement check until this closing process has concluded and the paperwork has been signed.

Case Study: Increasing Your Settlement

Hiring an experienced personal injury lawyer may substantially increase your recovery, even if there is limited money available from insurance policies. To illustrate, here's an example of how a personal injury lawyer's negotiations made a difference for one client who was injured in a motorcycle accident.

The client in this case, a woman in her twenties, was riding on the back of her boyfriend's motorcycle when a tire fell off the back of a tow truck and struck the motorcycle. She was seriously injured in the resulting accident, with medical bills reaching a total of $140,000. The tow truck's insurance company offered her $100,000, which it claimed was the total amount available under the insurance policy covering the tow truck. That is, that was what they claimed before she retained a lawyer. Before calling a lawyer, she had worked out an agreement with her medical providers, in which they would receive the entire $100,000 available under the insurance policy, and she would make payments for the remaining amounts due over time.

After the woman hired an experienced personal injury lawyer, she was pleased to learn that she could obtain more compensation. The lawyer was able to locate the existence of another insurance policy with an additional $300,000 in coverage. Furthermore, the lawyer was able to use certain defenses under the law to avoid paying back the woman's health insurance carrier for the medical bills the plan had paid. As a result, the woman received more than $100,000 in her pocket after her fees, costs, liens and healthcare expenses were deducted from the settlement recovery. Not a bad result for picking up the phone and asking an experienced personal injury attorney for help.

Chapter Seven: Trial

Once you have been through all of the detailed preparations for a jury trial, you might see why most people prefer not to go to court. People want their disputes solved quickly and fairly. While a trial may be fair, it is rarely quick. A trial requires months of preparation, even if the trial only lasts a few days in court.

The good news is that many cases handled by experienced personal injury lawyers are settled long before litigation would have started. And in most cases where a lawsuit is filed, the parties still settle before going to the courtroom. It is the collective experience of the lawyers collaborating on this book that 95% or more of personal injury cases handled by an experienced personal injury lawyer settle well before trial. However, your lawyer will never know in the beginning whether your case falls into that 5% of cases that will go to court. So every case has to be prepared with the anticipation that a trial may be necessary. Ironically, those cases that are thoroughly prepared for trial end up having the best chances of settling without having to go to trial.

An experienced personal injury lawyer will prepare your case, from the beginning, just as if it will ultimately go to court. This is not just in case you do go to trial — it is also because full preparation allows you and your lawyer to make the most compelling case possible in settlement talks. The facts will be gathered. The witnesses will be found. Experts may be hired. The evidence will be assimilated. The issues will be understood. The law will be applied to the facts. Demands for settlement will be presented. Mediation or other alternative dispute resolution methods may have been utilized and failed. The last step is trying the case before a jury of your peers.

Sometimes You Have to Go to Trial

Sometimes, a trial is necessary in order to reach a fair settlement. That was the case for one 59-year-old man who was badly hurt when hit while crossing the street in a marked crosswalk. He was in the hospital for more than two weeks, and then stayed at a nursing care facility for more than three months. The man's medical bills exceeded $120,000.

To the man's lawyers, it appeared to be a clear case of negligence — the other driver failed to slow or otherwise stop for a person in a marked cross walk. But the defendant driver denied liability, and his insurance company argued that witnesses said the injured man darted into the street without checking for traffic. The last offer before trial was $50,000—not even enough to pay for the medical bills. The man's lawyer spent nearly two years performing discovery, deposing witnesses, and talking to the man's doctors about the extent of his client's injuries. After mediation failed, the lawyer tried the case to a 12-person jury. After a six-day trial, the jury returned with a verdict of about $787,000.

The Complaint and Answer

In Washington, every lawsuit starts with a written complaint filed in court by the plaintiff's lawyer. The plaintiff's complaint lays out all of the relevant facts, then lists each cause of action (the legal reason for suing), and then requests or prays for an award of damages. The person or other party being sued is called the defendant. A copy of the complaint must be personally served on each defendant, along with a summons which instructs the defendant how and when to respond to the complaint.

The defendant responds to the complaint by filing a document called an answer. Each defendant either admits or denies all of the allegations raised in the complaint. Together, the complaint and answer will often frame the issues presented in the lawsuit.

Motions

Once the case is filed in court, either side is free to file a motion. A motion is a formal request to the judge asking that a ruling be made on some issue in the case. For example, a defendant may move to dismiss the complaint by asking the court to rule that the complaint was filed too late (the complaint was not filed within the statute of limitations period).

There are different standards of review that may apply to a particular motion. In some motions, the judge may be forced to accept as true the other party's allegations for purposes of ruling whether the motion should be granted or not. In other cases, like a summary judgment motion, the judge must determine whether there are sufficient material facts in dispute to allow the case to go to trial. Still other motions may merely ask the judge to weigh the evidence and arguments presented by both sides and then exercise discretion on an appropriate remedy or decision.

Motions are an important part of the litigation and trial process. Often times, each side's motion practice is focused on keeping certain evidence away from the jury or permitting certain evidence to come in. A lawyer's effective motions practice can have a significant effect on the likelihood of success in any given legal case.

Jury and Bench Trials

When your lawyer files the complaint, either side may request that the case be decided by a jury. Many courts require that a separate document be submitted to the court along with a jury fee paid to the clerk. In this author's experience, most defense attorneys will ask for a jury demand because it can be more difficult to persuade twelve (12) ordinary citizens than just one judge. A jury consists of a group of randomly selected citizens from your area who are summoned to court for jury selection. Usually the jurors are selected from voter registration and driver license records.

After all evidence is presented, the jury will use directions from the judge (called jury instructions) to decide the three most important questions in any civil trial: fault (or negligence), causation and damages. Questions of fault ask the jury to decide whether each defendant was negligent (or careless). Questions of causation ask the jury to decide whether the defendant's negligence was a proximate cause of the plaintiff's injuries and/or damages. Then the jury is asked to decide the amount of the plaintiff's damages caused by the defendant's negligence.

And finally, if there is more than one defendant, or if there is a question about whether the plaintiff was also negligent, the jury is asked to decide what percentage of fault should be assigned to each of the parties.

The judge who presides over a trial (also called the court) is responsible for deciding issues of law in the case, and to make sure each side is allowed to present their side of the case in accordance with applicable law. A judge's job is to decide what evidence is admissible by deciding pre-trial motions (also called *motions in limine*) and ruling on objections by the lawyers. In essence, the judge acts like a referee during the course of trial to make sure that each side's rights are protected, and that each side gets to present their version of the case within the rules of evidence.

Burden of Proof

As the party seeking financial damages, the plaintiff has the burden of proof. This means that the plaintiff has the burden of proving each and every element of each cause of action before a recovery can be made. There are different levels of the burden of proof. Most people are familiar with "proof beyond a reasonable doubt," which is the highest burden of proof that exists and applies in a criminal case. However, in civil cases like those dealing with personal injury claims, the burden of proof is significantly lower. That burden is a "preponderance of the evidence," which means that the level of proof must be more likely true than not. Some attorneys claim that it is the 51% burden of proof, because the plaintiff need only tip the scales (i.e., 51% vs. 49%) in the plaintiff's favor to win the case.

Presenting and Defending the Case

Because the plaintiff has the burden of proof, your lawyer gets to present your case first during trial. After your lawyer has presented all of the evidence in support of your claim, or has "rested," then the defendant gets to present his evidence or side of the case.

Each side has the right to present witnesses and other evidence, like exhibits. There usually is no limit to the number of witnesses may be called, as long as each person offers new and relevant testimony, or testimony that is not considered cumulative or that wastes the court's time. Each side also gets to cross-examine the other party's witness by asking leading questions. An effective cross examination can have a very powerful effect on the jury and can often help win or lose a case.

After both parties have rested, either side may then present "rebuttal" evidence or testimony that specifically attempts to rebut or refute the other side's evidence on a specific issue or point. This means that additional witnesses or pieces of evidence may be presented to the jury after each side rests their case.

At some point during or near the end of trial, the judge and each party's lawyer will address and argue the written instructions that will be given to the jury. This is always done outside of the presence of the jury. Each party's lawyer has the opportunity to submit their own set of instructions for the judge to review and consider. The instructions are supposed to be concise and accurate statements of the law for the type of claim before the jury. The judge is usually given substantial discretion to decide which instructions to use. Sometimes the attorneys may argue over whether a simple word or sentence in a jury instruction is proper. Once argument over the instructions has been considered by the court, the judge decides which instructions will to go to the jury. Drafting and arguing which jury instructions go to the jury is an extremely important part of the trial. The difference of a word, or how a particular phrase or sentence is written, can make a huge difference in the outcome of a trial.

After jury instructions have been decided by the judge, the attorneys for each side are permitted to make their closing statements to the jury. But first the court's instructions are read to the jurors before the attorneys are allowed to make their final summations. In Washington, the rules governing closing statements in civil trials are quite broad. Unless the lawyer's statements are clearly prejudicial, or if they violate one of the judge's earlier rulings about which evidence is admissible, the lawyers are given wide latitude to argue their theory of the case.

Since the plaintiff has the burden of proof, he gets to close first. Then the defense lawyer makes his or her closing statement. And finally, the plaintiff's lawyer gets to make a rebuttal closing. Only the plaintiff's lawyer gets to make a rebuttal closing statement since the plaintiff is the party that has the burden of proof.

The Jury Verdict

After all the evidence has been submitted, both sides have rested, the court's instructions are read to the jury, and closing statements have concluded, the jury will be asked to deliberate the case. The jury's deliberation is in secret and outside the presence of the judge, the lawyers and the parties. In theory, the jury is supposed to decide which set of facts were proven true and then apply the law (the court's instructions) to those facts. In Washington, only 10 out of 12 jurors need to agree upon a verdict.

If the jury cannot reach a verdict by a 10 to 2 margin, the court will declare a mistrial (also called a "hung jury"). When a trial ends with a hung jury, the case has to be retried before a new jury, starting from the beginning. Plaintiff lawyers usually do not like hung juries because it means the case has to be retried at significant expense.

New Trial

What if you don't like the jury's verdict? Can a new trial be ordered? Yes, but only in very limited circumstances. In Washington, there are only a handful of reasons which may allow a judge to order a new trial. There is a very strong presumption that a jury's verdict is correct and should stand. Some of the reasons which might support a new trial are that the evidence does not support the verdict, or that an error of law was committed during the trial, or that the jury violated one of the court's instructions while in deliberation. Absent these unusual facts, the jury's verdict will almost always stand.

Judgment and Collection

Once the jury renders its verdict, it will be reduced to judgment. This just means a separate piece of paper will be filed setting forth the amount of money the defendant must pay to the plaintiff. Most of the time the defendant will have insurance and the carrier will promptly pay the judgment (practically speaking the defendant will almost always have insurance because most plaintiff attorneys will not work on a case unless there is a guaranteed source of recovery).

If there is no insurance or not enough insurance, the plaintiff may start collection efforts. Some of these efforts include procedures such as collecting from the person's wages or a bank account (called a writ of garnishment). Another procedure is to seize property and try to sell it to pay off the judgment (called a writ of execution). However, these collection efforts are time-consuming and will likely result in additional attorney fees and expenses.

One problem with trying to execute on a judgment by going after the defendant's personal funds or assets is that the defendant can declare bankruptcy. If this happens, the bankruptcy proceeding can suspend all collection efforts and then discharge the underlying judgment debt. If the judgment debt is discharged, then the judgment will not have to be paid in full. This is why most cases should be settled for the defendant's insurance policy limits without having to go to trial if those limits are tendered by the insurance carrier. It costs a lot of money just in court costs and other expenses to try a case to verdict and then judgment. This significant expense must be borne by the client. So unless the defendant is incredibly wealthy (worth millions), it does not make sense to go to trial for the purpose of trying to collect more than defendant's insurance policy limits. If you do decide to go after the defendant's personal assets there is no guarantee of recovering more money. And the entire judgment debt may be discharged if the defendant decides to declare bankruptcy.

Appeals

If the judge refuses a request to order a new trial, either side may appeal the jury's verdict. To win the appeal, you generally must show that the judge made an error of law which substantially prejudiced the other side's right to a fair trial. For instance, an appeal won't succeed just because you think the jury's verdict was wrong or unfair. Statistically, the chance that an appeal will succeed is less than 25-30% of the time.

In Washington, the appeal is first heard by the Court of Appeals. There are three separate divisions of the Court of Appeals. Each division is a separate court made up of three judges who review the trial record to make sure the trial judge made the correct rulings and that neither side was prejudiced unfairly in violation of the law. This court cannot hear new evidence or make a judgment on the evidence that was submitted below in the trial court (unless it was wrongly admitted). Appeals are labor intensive as well. The party who appeals is responsible for transcribing the entire record and submitting it to the court and the other parties. This can be a significant expense. There are also additional attorney fees to handle the appeal to conclusion. An appeal in Washington can also take a long time to conclude, usually at least 18 to 24 months after the appeal has been filed.

Once the Court of Appeals issues its decision, either side can then appeal to the Washington State Supreme Court. But an appeal to the state supreme court is not automatically heard. The Washington Supreme Court can exercise its discretion on whether to hear the appeal or not. Usually the Supreme Court will only hear an appeal if there is a constitutional issue presented, or if there is a difference of opinions between the three appellate divisions on an important issue. To appeal to the state Supreme Court you must present a "petition for discretionary review." This is a separate document where you try to persuade the court to accept your appeal. Most petitions for discretionary review to the state Supreme Court are denied.

It Is the Client's Case

Some potential clients are afraid that a lawyer will make important decisions about their cases. These decisions may include deciding the settlement amount without input from the client, or the decision to file a lawsuit or not. Yet these fears are unfounded, at least in this author's office. Davis Law Group believes a personal injury claim belongs at all times to the client. We will certainly guide the client and make recommendations, but the ultimate decision to settle or go to court remains with the client. At Davis Law Group we know that litigation is a means to an end, not the end itself. Our purpose, whether achieved through litigation or settlement, is to obtain justice for the client. That means recovering full and fair financial compensation for the client and holding negligent wrongdoers responsible for their actions. In the end, Davis Law Group is here to serve the client to the best of our abilities, and we have been successfully doing that for the last 16+ years.

Conclusion

I wrote this book to give the reader a helpful and relatively detailed guide to the personal injury claims and litigation process, and to answer relatively common questions my office receives from potential clients. I believe the information in this book is important for those of you who have already decided to pursue a case, as well as those individuals who simply want to learn more about their rights and remedies after getting injured through little or no fault of their own.

Yet I know that no book can ever address and answer every possible question or set of circumstances that may arise in any one case. In fact, two cases that appear similar on the surface may involve widely different issues or problems that are unique to that plaintiff. That is why the reader should at least consult with an experienced personal injury attorney before pursuing the claim on his own, especially if the injuries are serious and the damages are significant.

We at the Davis Law Group believe passionately in what we do; that is, helping accident victims understand their rights and then helping them navigate through the personal injury claims minefield. Most accident victims are surprised to learn that once they enter the claims process it is much like a war zone. The insurance companies who try to defeat or minimize the claim go to extraordinary lengths to accomplish these goals. If you are an accident victim, you really need an experienced advocate on your side; a firm with a proven track record of success and one that has attorneys who are above reproach in their honesty and integrity. We call this the Davis Law Group Advantage—we go to extraordinary lengths to protect your rights and if necessary go head-to-head with the insurance company and its lawyers and experts. You won't be outgunned no matter what they throw at you.

I hope this book has answered many of your questions and concerns. And I hope it also has helped you better understand the personal injury claims process and what you can expect if litigation is necessary. If you feel that you would like the benefit of the Davis Law Group Advantage, please feel free to contact us at the number below. We will do our best to help in any way we can.

Davis Law Group, P.S.
2101 Fourth Avenue, Suite 1030
Seattle, WA 98121
Phone (206) 727-4000
Fax (206) 727-4001
DavisLawGroupSeattle.com

About The Author

 Washington attorney Christopher Michael Davis has been representing children and adults in accident cases and against insurance companies since 1994. In 2006, he was named a Rising Star Attorney by Washington Law & Politics magazine (a recognition given only to the top 2.5% of lawyers age 40 and under in Washington State).

Since 2007, and each year thereafter, Washington Law & Politics named Mr. Davis a Super Lawyer (the top 5% of all lawyers in Washington). Mr. Davis has also been named in the "Top 100 Trial Lawyers" in the State of Washington by the American Trial Lawyers Association each year since 2007.

As a firm, Davis Law Group was recently named the "Best Personal Injury Law Firm" in Washington State as part of Acquisition International's 2016 Dispute Resolution Awards.

Mr. Davis speaks at Continuing Legal Education seminars on topics related to personal injury. He teaches and instructs other lawyers in Washington State on topics such as jury selection, proving damages and developing winning trial techniques.

Mr. Davis has written and published several articles and books about personal injury law, the claims process, trial techniques, and other valuable information for accident victims and other plaintiff lawyers. He has also been asked by Mothers Against Drunk Driving (MADD) to write legal briefs on its behalf when the Washington appellate courts are asked to decide legal issues involving drunk driving offenses and how they are prosecuted.

Mr. Davis has been licensed to practice law in Washington State since 1993. He has obtained millions of dollars in verdicts and settlements for his clients. He has successfully represented hundreds of adults and children in serious accident cases involving traumatic brain injury, paralysis, and wrongful death. Mr. Davis is also a member of numerous professional organizations, including Super Lawyers, The Washington State Association for Justice, The American Association for Justice, American Lawyer Academy, and the North American Brain Injury Society.

For a sampling of verdicts and settlements achieved by Mr. Davis in a variety of cases, please visit DavisLawGroupSeattle.com.

DAVIS LAW GROUP, P.S.
2101 Fourth Avenue, Suite 1030
Seattle, WA 98121
Phone: 206-727-4000
Fax: 206-727-4001
DavisLawGroupSeattle.com

·